# QUALITATIVE ASSESSMENT OF TEXT DIFFICULTY

# Qualitative Assessment of Text Difficulty

## A Practical Guide for Teachers and Writers

Jeanne S. Chall
Glenda L. Bissex
Sue S. Conard
Susan H. Harris-Sharples

**BROOKLINE BOOKS**

Cover design, book design and typography by Erica L. Schultz.

ISBN 1-57129-023-0

**Library of Congress Cataloging-In-Publication Data**
Qualitative assessment of text difficulty : a practical guide for
  teachers and writers / Jeanne S. Chall ... [et al.]
    128 p.        cm.
    Includes bibliographical references (p. 104) and index (p. 107).
    ISBN 1-57129-023-0 (pbk.)
    1. Textbooks--Readability.  2. Readability (Literary style)
  I. Chall, Jeanne Sternlicht, 1921–      .
  LB3045.8.Q35    1996
  371.3'2--dc20                                        96-24405
                                                          CIP

Published by
**BROOKLINE BOOKS**
P.O. Box 1047
Cambridge, Massachusetts 02238-1047
Order toll-free: 1-800-666-BOOK

To Edgar Dale

*1902-1985*


Scholar, teacher, writer,
pioneer in
readability assessment
and clear writing

# CONTENTS

# PREFACE

It was Edgar Dale, when I was his graduate student and research assistant, who suggested that I might do something useful for writers of health materials. They need to know, even before they start to write, he said, what a piece of writing would look like if it were written for readers of a given level of reading ability. He further noted that while readability formulas were useful for assessing the difficulty of text after it is written, they were not as helpful in knowing how to start writing to reach a particular audience.

I pursued this idea for my Master's thesis (Chall, 1947) and developed a set of passages of increasing difficulty for writers of health materials. The passages were excerpted, with no changes, from books, pamphlets, and magazines. The difficulty levels ranged from 3rd grade to college graduate level, and were standardized using expert judgment and the tested comprehension of a group of readers.

These passages were included in a guide for writers of health materials (Dale & Hager, 1950). Similar scales were developed by Edgar Dale and myself for writers and editors of a children's encyclopedia.

Perhaps of equal value from my first study of reading scales was the finding that different methods of estimating difficulty tend to produce similar results. That is, tested reading comprehension, judgments of teachers, judgments of readers, and scores from readability formulas on the same materials produced essentially the same estimates of the difficulty of the texts. Thus, whether judgment, tested comprehension or a readability formula was used, the results regarding comprehension difficulty were quite similar.[1]

It has always been in the back of my mind to develop a more comprehensive procedure for using judgment to estimate reading difficulty. An opportunity came in the early 1970s when Edgar Dale and I again took up our long-standing dialogue as to whether we should or should not revise our readability formula (Dale & Chall, 1948). We were well aware that our formula, although widely used for several decades and considered to be the most reliable and valid of such formulas (Klare, 1963, 1984), had many weaknesses. Indeed, a survey of users conducted soon after it was first published and a comprehensive review of readability research and its applications ten years after the formula was published (Chall, 1956, 1958) suggested several areas that needed improvement. Time and other responsibilities kept us from undertaking a revision at that time.

By 1975 we had made a decision to go in two seemingly different directions: the first, toward improving the existing quantitative, objective measure, and the second, toward developing a more qualitative measure of readability (see Chall, 1958). The

---

[1] See Chall and Conard (1991); Stenner, Horabin, Smith and Smith (1988); and Smith, Stenner, Horabin and Smith (1989).

first task, a revised Dale-Chall formula, was undertaken with Edgar Dale (Chall & Dale, 1995). The second task focused on the use of qualitative judgments—a method that would make use of the intuitive knowledge of teachers, writers, and editors, and that would be easy to use.

For the task of developing a qualitative approach to readability, I was joined by three of my then doctoral students. All four of us participated in the initial planning and validation studies. In addition, each of my three co-authors took major responsibility for one of the content areas: Glenda Bissex for literature and popular fiction; Sue Conard for social studies; and Susan Harris-Sharples for science.

Geraldine Clifford (1978) noted that readability and vocabulary research has tended to be passed on from teacher to student. Indeed, this book has, in a sense, been just that—the product of three generations of scholars: my teacher, Edgar Dale; myself; and my students.

Soon after our work started, we realized that the time for a qualitative assessment had indeed come. In recent years, there has been a growing use of holistic scoring to assess student writing (Chall, Jacobs & Baldwin, 1990) and to estimate the readability of texts (Carver, 1975-76; Singer, 1975). The work took many years to complete, to validate and to prepare for publication. The qualitative procedure we developed was used experimentally for many years, including estimating the difficulty of textbooks analyzed for the study *An Analysis of Textbooks in Relation to Declining SAT Scores* (Chall, Conard, & Harris, 1977). Later it was used to assess the difficulty of about 800 literature and popular fiction books in the Harvard Reading Laboratory. The passages have also been used in graduate classes and teacher education workshops to introduce teachers to the developmental changes in reading from grade 1 to college graduate level.

Many have helped us with this project. We wish to thank Marcus Lieberman, our statistical consultant, for his always warm and joyful help; Susan Robinson and Isabel Phillips for their assistance in assessing the books in the Harvard Reading Laboratory; Andrea Kotula and Mary Lawler for their assistance in locating appropriate passages for the scales; Ruth Litchfield for reading and reacting to an early draft; and the many teachers, graduate students, and children who participated in the standardization of the passages. We also acknowledge the assistance of Gail Kearns in the testing of the passages and Anne Cura and Sharon Hibbert for their care in preparing the manuscript.

The work is dedicated to the memory of Edgar Dale for his inspiration, long years of encouragement, and generous assistance. In a real sense, he started me on this kind of assessment more than forty years ago. He was a pioneer in readability measurement, an ingenious scholar of vocabulary difficulty, and a serious contributor to both the art and science of clear writing. Although he devoted his academic life to the study of objective means of measuring readability and vocabulary difficulty, he was himself an artist of clarity and grace in writing, and taught others to be the same.

This book is also dedicated to Sue Conard, a former student, research assistant, colleague and co-author on this and other research projects. She passed away in 1992, after this book was nearly completed. We are grateful for her scholarship, her dedication, and friendship.

— *Jeanne Chall*
*Cambridge, MA*

# Part I
# Methods and Uses

# CHAPTER 1

# A Method for the Qualitative Assessment of Texts

This book presents a method for the qualitative assessment of text difficulty—a method that relies on a total impression rather than on an analysis of text features. The method is based on matching samples of text to exemplars that have been scaled for comprehension difficulty. These exemplars range in difficulty from those suitable for the reading ability of first graders to those requiring the most advanced, sophisticated level of reading ability—typically suitable for college graduates.

The use of qualitative assessment rather than precise measurement has a long history in psychological and educational research. It has been used in the assessment of student writing (Chall, Jacobs, & Baldwin, 1990) and also in the assessment of text difficulty (see the Preface).

That qualitative assessments can be valid has been known for more than 80 years in psychological and educational research (see E.L. Thorndike's writing scale, 1910 and 1912). The evidence for qualitative assessment has been particularly strong for language and reading. Thus Shapiro (1967) found that adult subjects' estimates of the frequency of words correlated .9 with the frequencies found on the Thorndike-Lorge list (1944). Porter and Popp (1975) found a correlation of .8 between judgments of difficulty of children's books and the difficulty of those books as measured by cloze scores and oral reading errors. Still earlier, Chall (1958) found a .8 correlation between judges' ratings of the difficulty of passages and their readability levels (see also Auerbach, 1971; Popp & Lieberman, 1977).

## Whole Language and Reading Recovery

Qualitative assessment has been of even greater interest in the past decade. The use of portfolios as a means of assessing student status and development relies strongly on teacher and student judgment. The current wide use of literature and expository trade books for reading and language instruction has given rise to various qualitative schemes for assessing the difficulty of texts appropriate for students.

The Reading Recovery Program at Ohio State University has developed a list of titles for the early grades based on recommendations from New Zealand's Reading Recovery program and the results of field tests with Reading Recovery teachers using the books with children in the United States (*The Running Record, A Newsletter for Reading Recovery Teachers*, Spring 1992, p. 6). As new books become available, they are "leveled" against this basic list of books and with trial use by children and teachers.

The Ohio State Reading Recovery Booklist is organized along a maximum of 20 levels, ranging in complexity from simple caption texts to stories similar to those found in first grade readers. Levels are only approximate indicators of text difficulty and are intended to serve as a guide for the Reading Recovery teacher in the selection of the new book. Text features that influence the choice of a level for a particular book include: content in relation to children's personal experiences and interests; repetition of language patterns; vocabulary; illustration support for the meaning of the text; narrative style; and the size and placement of the print.

(*Reading Recovery Booklist*, August 1990, p. 2)

A scheme for leveling books for the first three grades by Weaver (1992) is also qualitative and based on the work done in New Zealand. Similar to the Ohio State Reading Recovery system, it takes account of content, language, and physical features of the text. At the grade three level, reference is made to the use of a readability formula.

Overall, the characteristics of difficulty used by the Reading Recovery Program at Ohio State and by Weaver are quite similar to those used in classic studies of readability since the 1930s. See, for example, Gray and Leary's *What Makes a Book Readable* (1935), and Chall and Dale (1995).

Why does qualitative evaluation of written language work so well? Perhaps it is the deep linguistic information that comes from a long, shared experience with language. Indeed, most teachers and writers, by virtue of their long experience with language, become ever more sensitive to its uses, and its relative difficulty. Still another advantage of qualitative assessment is its simplicity. It takes a fraction of the time taken by the quantitative measures.

Qualitative procedures for assessing text difficulty can be more sensitive to the overall difficulty of a text than measures based on text features alone. There are always limits to the text features that can be analyzed. Whether an assessment focuses on word or sentence features or on organization and cognitive features, it leaves out some important variables. Qualitative assessment can be more sensitive to the great variety of text variables that differentiate texts, including vocabulary, syntax, conceptual load, text structure, and cohesion (see Chall & Dale, 1995).

The qualitative method avoids some of the shortcomings of objective measures of text difficulty—particularly since the objective measures cannot include all of the factors known to predict difficulty. The classic readability formulas tend to focus on semantic and syntactic measures, while the new cognitive-structural readability procedures focus on idea difficulty, density, and organization (Chall & Dale, 1995). A qualitative assessment, because it is based on a total reaction to the text, can take account of these and other factors known to be associated with difficulty. Further, when qualitative assessments focus on different content areas, they make more transparent what actually happens as writing becomes more difficult to read and understand. Thus, use of this procedure educates the user while assessing the text.

We decided early that we would develop sets of scaled passages for the major content areas—literature, science and social studies. This decision was based on research findings in reading comprehension and readability indicating that the different content areas are sufficiently different in the demands they make on the reader to warrant the use of some reading skills that are relatively unique for each (Herber & Nelson-Herber, 1993). Further, those using the scales are likely to gain a fuller understanding of the nature of that text and of its comprehension demands than they would have gained from using quantitative measures of difficulty. (See Chapters 5, 6, and 7.)

The search for selections of superior quality also indicated important differences in the six scales. We found, as others have found, that the hardest passages were in the sciences. We were able to find many good selections at a college graduate level. The two scales for social studies varied, the narrative passages being considerably easier than the expository. We found good narrative passages that ranged from reading level 1 to reading level 11-12. We found none at college and college graduate levels.

The two kinds of fiction, literature and popular fiction, also varied, with the literature selections reaching a college level but the popular fiction only a 9-10 level. The popular fiction scales were the easiest of the six scales. (See p. 4 for further discussions of the different demands of the different content areas.)

The qualitative method of appraisal described in the following chapters also makes use of the intuitive knowledge of those for whom it is intended—teachers, writers, editors, and others who select, write, or assess materials for readers of given characteristics. It does not require counting text features. Instead, it matches samples of texts to exemplars scaled on the basis of teacher and student judgments, cloze comprehension tests, and other assessments.

The scales have many uses. They can be used for estimating the comprehension difficulty of text—that is, connected reading material—without counting text features and making computations to arrive at a reading difficulty score. Such reading materials can be found in instructional materials on a variety of topics; in trade books (fiction and/or non-fiction books that are used for an individual's pleasure and information, and increasingly used for instruction); in newspaper and magazine articles; and in "paper-and-pencil" test items, particularly reading tests. This simpler, qualitative approach is particularly appropriate for writers, editors, and teachers who seek a quick estimate of text difficulty. It is also useful for those who prepare reading materials for children and adults of given levels of reading ability.

The scales have still another use that is not directly concerned with assessing text ease or difficulty. They can be used for introducing teachers and parents to the processes involved in learning to read and becoming an ever more efficient reader. We discovered this use in the process of validating the passages for each of the content areas—literature, science, and social studies. Each of the teachers was asked to sort a given set of selections in order of increasing difficulty, and then discuss her rankings with one of the researchers. It was during these discussions that we became aware that the teachers discussed the changes in text difficulty not only in terms of text features (vocabulary, syntax, concepts, organization, etc.) but also in terms of the reader's ability and understanding that would be needed to match the textual changes. Thus— by gaining understanding as to how the reading selections change, level by level—teachers, parents, and writers can become sensitive to what students need to know and be able to do as they advance in their ability to read increasingly more difficult texts.

The scales are particularly useful now when more teachers are using trade books in addition to or in place of textbooks in the teaching of reading, language, science and social studies. Most textbooks are "graded" by their publishers. Trade books, however, usually carry only suggestions regarding their appropriateness for different ages. The qualitative, easy-to-use assessment scheme presented here will, we hope, fill the gap in selecting and writing trade books that are appropriate in difficulty for their targeted readers. It provides a quick assessment that gives assurance to teachers, writers and editors that their intuitive judgments are valid.

The scales are also useful to teachers of the three subject areas, to give them insight into how the reading materials in these areas—literature, social studies, and science—change as they become more difficult to read and comprehend; how student knowledge, skills, and abilities need to develop in order to read and understand the increasingly more difficult selections; and how materials differ by subject area at the same level. The qualitative method:

1. Offers an easy-to-use method for judging the difficulty of written texts, relying on qualitative judgments rather than on counting text features.
2. Presents to writers, teachers, and parents exemplars from literature, social studies, and science that can be read with comprehension at specific levels of proficiency.
3. Describes and illustrates changes in vocabulary, syntax, concepts, structure, and other features in materials that range in difficulty from a first grade level to a college graduate level.
4. Provides a reliable and valid method for estimating difficulty which compares favorably with expert teacher judgment of difficulty, student judgment of difficulty, and student reading comprehension. It also compares favorably with classic readability scores—and at a fraction of the time.
5. The scales provide an easy-to-use introduction to reading development for beginning teachers, parents, and others interested in reading development from its beginnings to its most mature forms.

# The Development of the Scales:
# Separate Scales for Different Domains

The use of scaled passages in each of a variety of domains and genres to assess text difficulty qualitatively is based on the considerable research evidence of the importance of schema or background knowledge in reading comprehension. It has long been accepted that reading in the different content areas requires different background knowledge and different strategies. Our further differentiation by genre is based on growing evidence that narrative is easier—both to read and to write—than is expository text.

For a long time, too, it has been suggested in the literature on reading instruction that reading in the different content areas requires different kinds of instruction (Herber, 1978; Herber & Nelson-Herber, 1993). Differences in difficulty by content area were found by Auerbach (1971) and later by Popp and Lieberman (1977) in their analyses of widely used standardized reading tests. The easier passages were narratives of familiar experiences, while the harder passages (above grade 4) were typically expository selections in social studies and science.

Recent as well as classic studies of reading comprehension in science and social studies have concluded that sufficient differences exist for reading in these domains to warrant special treatment. Indeed, the past decade has seen renewed interest in the special problems of reading within different content areas at both the upper-elementary and high school levels. For building literacy among adults, Sticht (1975, 1982) has called for the use of work-type instructional materials for individuals with limited reading ability, instead of concentrating only on general materials. There has also been a growing emphasis on teaching reading comprehension skills in particular content areas (Herber & Nelson-Herber, 1993).

Readability research has also made similar recommendations. Based on a review of the research and its applications, Chall (1958) suggested developing separate readability procedures for different subject areas. This recommendation came from evidence of the influence of different subject areas on reading comprehension and readability. As far as we know, no readability procedure has, so far, been developed for special content areas, with the exception of the health scales (Chall, 1947) noted in the preface.

Thus, based on the research in reading comprehension and readability, and on current trends in reading instruction, we decided to develop scales in three content areas—in literature, in science, and in social studies.

As our work proceeded, it became apparent that each content area should further be separated into two sets. Consequently, the literature passages were separated into a set of literature selections and a set of popular fiction selections; the science set was divided into scales for the life sciences and for the physical sciences; and the social studies set was divided into one set of narrative selections and another of expository prose, both on American history.

# Qualitative Changes in Texts: From Very Easy to Very Hard

An overview of the six scales will reveal that as the passages become more difficult, they change on several dimensions: in language, in concepts, and in the difficulty of thought. The changes in *language* are probably the most apparent. Generally, as one moves from the lowest to highest levels of difficulty, one finds changes in such linguistic features as vocabulary and syntax. Vocabulary changes from easy, familiar, highly frequent and usually short words to words that are less common, less frequent, less familiar, more abstract, technical, or literary. With increasing difficulty, sentences become longer, more complex, less direct, with greater embedding of ideas.

In most texts, as the vocabulary increases in difficulty, so does the complexity of the sentences. That is, in natural writing, when one writes about familiar ideas, one tends to use easier words and shorter, less complex, sentences. Difficult ideas are usually expressed in less familiar, more technical and abstract words, and more complex sentences.

Another dimension is that of the *density and difficulty of the ideas expressed*. The more difficult passages, in all the content areas, tend to contain more concepts that are less familiar and more abstract. They also assume that the reader has prior knowledge of most of these concepts.

A third dimension is that of *cognitive difficulty*. As the passages get more difficult, they require more thought, reasoning, analysis, and critical abilities to fully understand them. Thus, in the harder passages, the difficulty and concentration of ideas expressed require considerable analysis, inference, and critical awareness.

Overall, to read at ever higher levels it is necessary for the reader to cope with increasingly difficult language, concepts, and thought, as well as to have the prior knowledge assumed by the text. In addition, it is necessary to have the requisite reading skills—to recognize the words quickly, sound the unfamiliar words and names easily, and read fluently and at a good rate. Generally, the passages of greater difficulty require more advanced reading skills than the easier ones. Thus, although specific aspects of difficulty may differ from one content area to another, there is a core of reading, language, and cognitive abilities needed by the reader in order to read and understand texts of all kinds of content at ever higher levels.

Early on we found ourselves using the metaphor of an iceberg as we tried to express the increasing difficulty of the selections. Each passage came to represent the tip of an iceberg, beneath which were the various sources of difficulty—linguistic, conceptual, structural, cognitive, etc. The more difficult the passage, the greater the ice beneath.

## Scaling the Exemplar Passages

Books (trade books *and* textbooks) and magazines of high quality were selected to represent a wide range of difficulty within the three content areas. A large number of passages, more than were needed for the final scales, were selected. Their difficulty was assessed by a combination of several procedures: independent rankings of difficulty by the four researchers; independent rankings by several groups of teachers and reading specialists; comprehension difficulty as estimated by readability formulas; and also, for the expository social studies selections, cloze tests and students' judgments of difficulty. The passages selected for the exemplars were those on which there was greatest agreement using the various difficulty measures.

## Validating the Scales

To determine difficulty levels, the passages were compared with each other and with independent measures of difficulty. High agreement was found between the qualitative assessments, classic readability scores, and tested reading comprehension. See Chapter 8 for a full discussion of reliability and validity of the qualitative method.

## Format of the Passages

All of the passages are printed in the same size and style of type, in order to help judges concentrate on the language and cognitive aspects of the text. When large type and colorful illustrations are used with fairly difficult text, judges often rate the text as easier than it actually is. Therefore, for judging text difficulty and for writing at a specified level, we use passages in a uniform typeface and size.

To help those who may not be familiar with the overall appearance of texts at various levels of difficulty, we also present the exact reproductions for passages at reading levels 1, 2, 3 and 4 in Appendix A, p. 82. (We do not include those for reading levels 5-6 through 16+ because there is usually little difference in size or style of type or in illustrations for texts at these levels.)

When the photocopied book pages were used in preliminary tryouts, we found that some of the raters responded strongly to the size of type in making their estimates of difficulty. Porter and Popp (1975) also found this for children's trade books. In fact, they found size of type to be a significant factor in judging overall difficulty of children's trade books at first to fourth grade levels. Our preliminary tryouts indicated that when the photocopied examples were used, texts with large type received somewhat lower ratings of difficulty than found from other measures. We therefore used the uniformly printed versions of the passages for the standardization.

In all passages, the language was kept exactly as it was written by the authors. No adaptations or changes were made in any of the selections.

In summary, our goal was to develop an assessment method of use to teachers, writers, and editors who make frequent judgments about text difficulty and who are also called on to write at given reading levels. We sought to develop a method that uses the judges' intuitive knowledge and experience, that is reliable and valid, and that takes little time to use.

Although it was not our initial goal, we found that the series of scales was an effective tool for introducing beginning teachers, parents, and other lay people to an understanding of reading, how it develops, and what students need to learn to progress from the easiest to the most advanced stages of proficiency.

Chapter 2 presents the variety of uses of the qualitative assessment method. Chapter 3 contains detailed instructions for use of the qualitative assessment method. Chapter 4 presents the six scales: literature and popular fiction, two scales for science—one for life sciences and one for physical sciences, and two scales for social studies—one for narrative writing and one for expository writing. Chapters 5, 6, and 7 contain qualitative analyses and discussions of the six scales to give the reader insights into how the passages change as they become ever more difficult to read and comprehend. Chapter 8 contains evidence of the reliability and validity of the scales.

# CHAPTER 2

# Uses of the Qualitative Method

## For Assessment of Texts

Text difficulty has been a concern of educational researchers and practitioners for more than seventy years (Chall & Conard, 1991). Educational publishers have considered texts of appropriate difficulty to be one of the most important aspects of textbook development. Teachers and administrators have also considered the appropriate matching of textbooks and readers to be one of the most important factors in the successful use of text and trade books. Hence, over the years, publishers, writers, editors, and teachers have used various instruments to match the difficulty of texts to the reading abilities of readers (Chall & Conard, 1991; Chall & Dale, 1995; Conard, 1981; Harris-Sharples, 1983).

The new research on text difficulty confirms the old. For example, the National Assessment of Educational Progress (NAEP) Reading Report Card (1985) notes that the difficulty of the passage was one of the three most important factors in comprehension of 4th, 8th, and 12th graders. The other two factors were familiarity with the subject matter and the kinds of questions asked (Chall & Conard, 1991). More recently, Anderson (1992) found that the oral reading errors of 2nd and 3rd graders were influenced most by the reading difficulty (particularly the word difficulty) of selections they were asked to read.

Reading difficulty has been and continues to be one of the most important factors in reading comprehension. We believe, therefore, that a quick, qualitative way to measure readability should prove useful to writers, editors, and teachers.

Teachers can use the scales to understand what typical students are able to read, as well as those reading above or below grade level. It is important for teachers to realize that the passage levels are calibrated to *reading levels, not to grade placement.* There are large numbers of children who read one, two, or more levels above their grade placement; large numbers also read one or more levels below their placement. The levels used for the six scales are meant to be reading levels.

Librarians, too, can use the scales to help children and adults select books within their reading level, by asking them which passages in a scale contain the kind of writing they can read and understand. The level they select can be matched to available books.

Parents will find the scales useful as an aid to locating the books their children will find readable, and also as an illustration of how reading changes as it develops.

## As Exemplars for Writers and Editors

The passages can be used by writers, editors, and curriculum developers who write for students at particular levels. The scaled passages within the various content areas illustrate the kind of writing that can be read and understood by readers of different proficiencies (see Chapter 4). Writers—as well as teachers and parents—often ask what a 4th- or 7th-grade reading ability *means*. The scales can help give some explanation of this. A 4th-grade reading ability means the ability to read, with understanding, the passages within a reading level of 4 and below. With assistance, the next higher level may also prove readable. For independent reading, a somewhat lower level may be more appropriate.

If a writer intends to write a social studies article for students of about 8th-grade reading level, a study of the social studies passages at reading levels 7-8 can serve as a guide for the appropriate level of difficulty. Descriptions of the linguistic characteristics (the vocabulary and sentence characteristics) as well as the concepts, organization, and background knowledge required of readers provide additional information as to the kind of texts that will be understood by students reading at approximately this level. Social studies authors of both narrative and expository texts will find examples and descriptions of each genre. (See Chapters 4 and 7.)

Study of the passages is suggested as a way to prepare for writing. The actual writing is best done more creatively by keeping in mind one or two persons for whom one writes—their reading ability, what they already know about the topic, how interested they are in it, etc. The scales help the writer obtain a more concrete grasp of the language, complexity, and idea density suitable for individuals of different reading abilities.

The scales are particularly useful for writers because they are composed of authentic writing. The literature selections come from old and modern classics. The popular fiction passages are taken from publications of highly successful writers. The life science, physical science, and narrative and expository social studies selections are taken from textbooks, trade books, and magazines widely read by children, young people, and adults.

We did not develop our own selections or adapt selections from published books; we thought it important that the scales represent *published*, high-quality writing at each of the levels and within each content area. The passages were selected as examples of good writing at different levels of difficulty.

Publishers adapting texts from one reading level to another will find in the scaled passages, and in the analyses of their characteristics, factors beyond language changes that should be taken into account (see Chapters 5, 6, and 7). Merely breaking up longer sentences and simplifying vocabulary does not guarantee that reading materials will be completely appropriate for lower reading levels. For example, if background information that higher-level readers could be assumed to know was not supplied in a "simplified" science text, readers might still struggle to comprehend it.

# For Understanding Reading Development

We have used these sets of passages in pre-service and in-service teacher education to make explicit the developmental changes in reading. The passages provide teachers with an opportunity to closely study the demands that texts make upon readers as they progress from a first-grade reading level to the most advanced college-graduate level.

*Stages of Reading Development* (Chall, 1983, 1996) characterizes reading—as it develops from its beginnings through its most advanced forms—in terms of changes in readers, in the texts they are able to read, and in the depth of understanding expected. One of the ways to increase understanding of these progressive changes in readers and in texts is through close study of the six scales (Chapter 4) and the discussion and analysis of the scales (Chapters 5, 6, and 7).

Those preparing to be teachers, as well as those who already teach at the elementary and high school levels, can gain insight into what is meant by reading at ever higher levels. By immersing themselves in the scales, they can more fully appreciate why successive passages are more difficult to read and understand than the preceding ones, and they can understand what readers have to learn in order to advance to the next higher level of texts.

When experienced teachers and reading specialists were given sets of literature passages in random sequence and asked to arrange them in order of increasing difficulty, their judgments much more closely approximated the researchers' than did the judgments of young teachers in training. The rankings by experienced teachers and reading specialists varied no more than one level from ours, while rankings by teachers in training varied by two or occasionally three levels (especially on the more difficult passages), although most of the rankings did coincide with ours. The criterion they usually used was, "Which passage is easier/harder for me to read?" Probing what caused a passage to be easier or harder then led them both to analyze characteristics of the texts and to examine the knowledge that they, as readers, brought to the texts. Thus, the task of ranking the passages and explaining their judgments made them more aware of and articulate about sources of difficulty in reading.

While the scales may serve to confirm the intuitive and educated judgments of experienced teachers, they can also be used to pose problems that help pre-service teachers learn to analyze texts for difficulty and to understand how academic expectations and students' reading abilities develop.

Instructors of pre-service courses or in-service workshops for teachers might want to use this exercise with several sets of scaled passages. More discussion is generated when participants work in small groups to come up with an agreed-upon rank order. Participants could also be asked to find other books that match the passages in difficulty, perhaps creating collections of books for their classrooms on particular topics and at levels suitable for the widest range of reading abilities represented in their students. Searching for commonalities and differences among passages at the same reading levels but in different subject areas concretely demonstrates what "reading across the curriculum" means.

Teachers might then be asked, in light of their work with these passages, what they see as their responsibilities for teaching reading. They will need to consider such factors as:

- how they select reading materials
- what they expect students to comprehend from their reading
- how they ask students to demonstrate their understanding
- how they assess students' strengths and limitations as readers
- how they might help students capitalize on their strengths (for example, interest and knowledge on a particular topic) and overcome limitations (for example, insufficient technical vocabulary).

Whenever the goal is not merely to assess reading materials but to educate persons about the nature of comprehension difficulty in text, and thus increase their awareness and ability to judge independently, the scales provide a unique instrument.

Because the scales differentiate reading material by subject area and genre, they can help teachers construct reading profiles for individual students that reflect the way achievement varies with type of reading. Such profiles might raise questions such as whether a student reading at a lower level in social studies material than in a science text perhaps has more informational background in the latter subject than in the former. It may also indicate whether a reader is having difficulty shifting gears between the precision demanded in reading science and the ability to entertain ambiguity and multiple meanings that reading literature increasingly requires.

Content teachers can benefit from studying the scales, particularly those in their own area of specialization. There is general recognition that students in the intermediate grades of the elementary school and those in middle and high school need instruction and practice in reading in the different content areas. Reading of literature, science, and history are sufficiently different to warrant specific reading instruction in each, and they may require different difficulty levels for instruction.

The passage sets may also be of interest to children who are curious about what it means to learn to read. Children might enjoy reading the passages below their level to see how far they have come, and to try to read those above their level to measure themselves against what is to come.

We gained insights into children's views of reading difficulty from the responses of 2nd, 5th, and 8th graders, all proficient readers, whom we asked to rank-order expository social studies passages. Students in each grade were given one passage about one level below their reading ability, another on their level, and a third passage a level above. After the students ranked the three passages from easiest to hardest, we asked them why they thought some of the passages were more difficult than the others. These were some of their comments:

- *The second graders* spoke of the difficult passages as having too many "hard words." One child said that the hardest passage had "lots of words I couldn't sound out." Only one second grader, a child who was already fluent and read with very good comprehension, noted a lack of background knowledge as the cause of difficulty for the hardest passage.
- *The fifth graders* also talked about words as being the source of difficulty. However, for fifth graders, 'word difficulty' meant whether or not they knew the meanings of the words, rather than how hard or easy the words were to decode. Several said that their lack of background knowledge about the topic was the reason why some passages were difficult to read and understand.

- *The eighth graders*, for the most part, focused on a very different aspect of text difficulty. They said that the passages they found difficult did not stick to the topic. They preferred text that does not "ramble around" in details. They judged passages to be difficult to understand when the ideas were embedded in too many details. None of the eighth graders said that decoding was a problem, although a few mentioned not knowing what the words meant. One girl said that if she had known more about "civics stuff and history," the passages would have been easier for her to understand.

Thus, students' reasons for why text gets more difficult change with grade. For the younger students, difficulty in recognizing the words is the major reason they give for rating a passage hard. Second graders want to read text that contains words they can easily recognize or "sound out." Fifth graders want text that either uses words whose meanings they know or that provides definitions. They also have difficulty when the topic is not familiar. For the eighth graders, vocabulary and a linking of new information to their prior knowledge continues to be important. But in addition, they want text that provides ideas in a coherent manner, with a clear organizational structure for the main ideas and supporting details.

In a real sense, the comments of these students match what is known about reading development and about readability (see Chall's *Stages of Reading Development*, 1983, 1996, and Chall and Dale's 1995 review of the theories and research on readability).

The scales, thus, offer not merely a method for assessing text difficulty, but also serve as a window into the ways that texts and reading abilities develop. They provide an orientation to what the reading task is and what is expected of students in reading different texts at different levels.

# Part II
# Manual for Qualitative Assessment of Texts

# CHAPTER 3

# Instructions for Using the Qualitative Assessment Method

This chapter presents instructions for using the qualitative assessment method for assessing text difficulty. It also presents guidelines for matching text difficulty to prospective readers' abilities and their purposes for reading.

The passages presented in Chapter 4 are to be used for the qualitative assessments, because they are set in uniform type. Appendix A presents exact page reproductions of the literature passages for reading levels 1 to 4. However, these should not be used for making assessments.

## Specific Instructions for Assessing Difficulty

1. **Choose the Scale.** Decide which of the six scales is a most appropriate match with the materials you wish to assess—Literature or Popular Fiction; Life or Physical Sciences; or Narrative or Expository Social Studies. Select the set of passages that is closest in content and form to the material to be assessed.

2. **Select Samples for Assessment.** To estimate text difficulty, samples of the text are used. The entire text is used only for very short selections, e.g., test items, or ads. For books and articles, select approximately 100-word samples as follows:

   * *For books of 150 pages or longer*, select one sample from every 50th page. The first sample should be taken from the beginning section of the book (but not the first page), and systematically thereafter, from every 50th page.
   * For books, articles, or pamphlets *of 4 pages or less*, select 2 samples—one near the beginning and one near the end, but not exactly the beginning or end.

3. *Assess Difficulty of Samples.* Use the worksheet at the end of Chapter 3 (p. 18) to record assessments. Match each sample of text you wish to assess to the passages in the scale you have selected. Use the following procedures: The initial match should be qualitative, based on a total impression of text difficulty compared with the scaled passage it most resembles. This may be followed by comparing your sample to the following characteristics:

- *Language*—Vocabulary difficulty (unfamiliar, abstract, polysyllabic, and/ or technical words).
- *Sentence length and complexity.*
- *Conceptual difficulty*—The conceptual understanding required to comprehend the text, e.g.: the degree of abstractness; the amount of prior knowledge needed to understand the text.
- *Idea density and difficulty*—the number of ideas in the text and the difficulty of these ideas.

Additional guidelines for judging difficulty are found in Chapter 5 for literature and popular fiction; in Chapter 6 for life science and physical science; and in Chapter 7 for social studies (narrative and expository).

The difficulty of each sample should be assessed independently of those preceding or following.

On the worksheet, record your judgment of the difficulty level of each sample. Record interesting observations or doubts about a sample in the Comments column.

It should be noted that the scales are organized in an increasing order of difficulty. Each passage is given a reading level from 1 (a level that is generally within the reading ability of children in the second half of grade 1) to a reading level of 16+ (generally within the reading ability of college graduates). Reading levels beyond 4 are combined into bands—5-6 (5th and 6th reading level), 7-8 (7th and 8th reading levels), 9-10 (9th and 10th reading levels), 11-12 (11th and 12th reading level), 13-15 (college level), and 16+ (college graduate level).

We have found the use of bands for the higher reading levels to be more realistic, for in practice, it is very hard to differentiate reading levels in the higher ranges of difficulty. This practice has been used successfully in the original and new Dale-Chall formulas and in other widely used readability formulas.

4. **Determine the Difficulty of the Entire Text.** For an overall estimate of the difficulty of a book or article, obtain an average of the reading levels for the samples. (To obtain an average using the reading level bands, use the higher number of the band. Take an average. Then convert back to the appropriate band.)[1]

---

[1] For example: If four samples from a given book are found to be at reading levels 4, 7-8, 5-6, and 4 (respectively), their average would be taken as the average of 4, 8, 6, and 4—thus, 5.5, which is converted back into reading level 5-6.

- *Interpreting the Scores*—The reading levels can be used in two ways. First, they are a measure of relative difficulty. Thus, the higher the reading level of the text, the more it will require of the reader in terms of reading ability, prior knowledge, and thought. Generally, materials on lower levels will be easier to read than those on higher levels. Second, the reading levels can be "matched" to the readers' abilities and purposes in reading. Thus, when a text is found to be on a 5-6 reading level, students who read on these levels will probably find it within their reading ability—all other things being equal. Further, if they receive instruction from the teacher, they will find the text more accessible. If they read the material independently, it may be more difficult.

  A reader's reading ability can be estimated from his or her latest reading assessment—quantitative or qualitative. If this information is not available, it can be estimated by asking the student to look over a set of passages (social studies, science, or literature) and select those he or she would find readable. For a more exact match, the student may be asked to read the selected passage. For reading levels 1 through 4, the reading can be done orally. For reading levels 5-6 and above, the reading is better done silently, and some estimate obtained as to whether it was understood—e.g., telling or writing what it was about, or answering a few questions.

  It is important to note, however, that while estimates from the qualitative assessment method give valid and reliable judgments of text difficulty, they do not provide full information needed to determine optimal difficulty for individual readers. For such judgments, one needs to know more about the prospective readers: their reading abilities, background knowledge, and motivation for reading. Also, optimal text difficulty is dependent upon whether the texts will be used for instruction with teacher assistance, or for independent reading. Generally, when reading levels, background knowledge, and motivation are high, the printed material can be more difficult and still be optimal. If teacher guidance is given, the text, again, can be more difficult. If little teacher guidance is given, the text should be on—or perhaps below—the student's tested reading level.

# Worksheet for Qualitative Assessments

*J.S. Chall, G. Bissex, S. Conard, S. Harris-Sharples*

Title _____     Author _____

Publisher _____     Date of publication _____

**CHECK SCALE USED:**

_____ Literature     _____ Life Sciences     _____ Social Studies – Narrative

_____ Popular Fiction     _____ Physical Sciences     _____ Social Studies – Expository

| Sample | Location of Sample | | Reading Level (1 to 16+) | Comments |
|---|---|---|---|---|
| | Page | From... To... | | |
| 1 | | | | |
| 2 | | | | |
| 3 | | | | |
| 4 | | | | |
| 5 | | | | |

**AVERAGE READING LEVEL:** _____

**COMMENTS** on book as a whole:

_____

_____

_____

_____

**MATCHING MATERIAL TO AN *INDIVIDUAL* READER:**

Estimated reading ability of the prospective reader: _____

How material is to be used (check one):

_____ For independent reading

_____ With minimal teacher instruction

_____ With teacher instruction

Estimated text difficulty for reader's ability and purpose (check one):

_____ Suitable     _____ Hard     _____ Easy

**MATCHING MATERIAL TO A *GROUP* OF READERS:**

Estimated *average* reading ability of prospective group of readers: _____

Estimated *range* of ability: _____

How material is to be used (check one):

_____ For independent reading

_____ With minimal teacher instruction

_____ With teacher instruction

Estimated text difficulty for group's ability and purpose (check one):

_____ Suitable     _____ Hard     _____ Easy

# CHAPTER 4

# Six Scales for Making Qualitative Assessments

This chapter contains the six scales to be used for making qualitative assessments of reading difficulty. In order to keep the major focus on the language and ideas, all the selections are printed in a uniform type size and style, and without illustrations.

The six scales are presented in the following order: Literature, Popular Fiction, Life Sciences, Physical Sciences, Narrative Social Studies, and Expository Social Studies. Within each of the six content categories, passages are listed by reading level—from easiest (reading level 1) to hardest (college graduate level). It should be noted that some of the scales begin at reading level 2 and some end at a 9-10 or 11-12 reading level.

The scales are to be used according to the instructions given in Chapter 3. The analysis and discussions found in Chapters 5 (Literature and Popular Fiction), 6 (Life Sciences and Physical Sciences), and 7 (Narrative and Expository Social Studies) provide additional insights into the characteristics that distinguish easy from difficult materials.

The books and magazines from which the selections were taken are listed in the bibliography in Appendix C, pp. 98-103. They are not listed here in order that the assessments be made on the basis of the selections provided and not on a general familiarity with the book.

## Literature Scale

**Reading Level 1[1]**

A train! A train!
A train! A train!
Could you, would you,
on a train?

Not on a train! Not in a tree!
Not in a car! Sam! Let me be!

I would not, could not, in a box.
I could not, would not, with a fox.
I will not eat them with a mouse.
I will not eat them in a house.
I will not eat them here or there.
I will not eat them anywhere.
I do not like green eggs and ham.
I do not like them, Sam-I-am.

**Reading Level 2**

Jonathan pushed back the big iron pot and stood up.

There were no bears. But up the path came his father, carrying his gun. And with him were Jonathan's Uncle James and his Uncle Samuel, his Uncle John and his Uncle Peter. Jonathan had never in all his life been so glad to see the uncles.

"Jonathan!" said his father, "what a fright you have given us! Where have you been all this time?"

"Coming over Hemlock Mountain," said Jonathan in a small voice. And he ran right into his father's arms.

---

[1] The level refers to the difficulty appropriate for the average child in the middle to end of first grade. The levels for the passages that follow are also to be viewed as generally being suitable for readers halfway through a grade or halfway through the bands containing two or three grades. We have not attempted to make fine distinctions between levels, because what is known about assessing text difficulty does not support such practice. Generally, the research as well as practice has found that the most valid and reliable measures of text difficulty are based on rather broad categories.

# Literature Scale

Reading Level 3

For months I had been telling myself that I would never put the Magic Finger upon anyone again—not after what happened to my teacher, old Mrs. Winter.

Poor old Mrs. Winter.

One day we were in class, and she was teaching us spelling. "Stand up," she said to me, "and spell kat."

"That's an easy one," I said. "*K-a-t.*"

"You are a stupid little girl!" Mrs. Winter said.

"I am not a stupid little girl!" I cried. "I am a very nice little girl!"

"Go and stand in the corner," Mrs. Winter said.

Then I got cross, and I saw red, and I put the Magic Finger on Mrs. Winter good and strong, and almost at once...

Guess what?

*Whiskers* began growing out of her face! They were long black whiskers, just like the ones you see on a kat, only much bigger. And how fast they grew! Before we had time to think, they were out to her ears!

Reading Level 4

The wheelbarrow picked up speed, so quickly that it sort of kicked up like a whipped horse. I thought the handle was going to rip right out of my fingers.

"Hang on," I said.

"If I can," said Soup.

We were running now, full speed, smack down Sutter's Hill and heading full tilt toward the party. Ahead of us, the giant pumpkin bounced around inside the bin of the barrow. I felt like we'd stolen the moon.

"We're out of control!" yelled Soup.

"Turn it. Do anything, anything!"

"Can't."

The front door of the Baptist Church grew bigger and bigger, rushing toward us like a mad monster. My feet hardly touched the ground. I was too frightened to hang on much longer, yet frightened even more to let loose. Soup was screaming and so was I.

"Stop," wailed Soup.

From the street, there was one step up to the door of the Baptist Church. The door was closed.

# Literature Scale

**Reading Level 5-6**

"Brothers. What do you expect of me—to stand idly by while you burn my son? My son has brought death to none of us. The scratches he gave us are not on our bodies but our pride. Brothers. How if my son is burnt do I go back and face her who lives with me in my house? How do I look in the eyes of his sisters who think the rainbow arches over him? Brothers. It is easier for me to fight you all than go back and say that Cuyloga stood by and did nothing while his brothers in anger put his son to the fire."

With the quickness of Long Tail, the panther, he took his knife and cut the boy's thongs. Then he stood there waiting for the attack, but none came. The warriors were too astonished. They watched, sullen and yet fascinated by the drama. This was the great Cuyloga at his bravest that they looked upon, and none knew what he would do next.

**Reading Level 7-8**

All day Buck brooded by the pool or roamed restlessly about the camp. Death, as a cessation of movement, as a passing out and away from the lives of the living, he knew, and he knew John Thornton was dead. It left a great void in him, somewhat akin to hunger, but a void which ached and ached, and which food could not fill. At times when he paused to contemplate the carcasses of the Yeehats, he forgot the pain of it; and at such times he was aware of a great pride in himself—a pride greater than any he had yet experienced. He had killed man, the noblest game of all, and he had killed in the face of the law of club and fang. He sniffed the bodies curiously. They had died so easily. It was harder to kill a husky dog than them. They were no match at all, were it not for their arrows and spears and clubs. Thenceforward he would be unafraid of them except when they bore in their hands their arrows, spears, and clubs.

# Literature Scale

**Reading Level 9-10**

Looking upward, I surveyed the ceiling of my prison. It was some thirty or forty feet overhead, and constructed much as the side walls. In one of its panels a very singular figure riveted my whole attention. It was the painted figure of Time as he is commonly represented, save that, in lieu of a scythe, he held what, at a casual glance, I supposed to be the pictured image of a huge pendulum, such as we see on antique clocks. There was something, however, in the appearance of this machine which caused me to regard it more attentively. While I gazed directly upward at it (for its position was immediately over my own) I fancied that I saw it in motion. In an instant afterward the fancy was confirmed. Its sweep was brief, and of course slow. I watched it for some minutes somewhat in fear, but more in wonder. Wearied at length with observing its dull movement, I turned my eyes upon the other objects in the cell.

A slight noise attracted my notice, and, looking to the floor, I saw several enormous rats traversing it. They had issued from the wall which lay just within view to my right.

**Reading Level 11-12**

For the rest he lived solitary, but not misanthropic, with his books and his collection, classing and arranging specimens, corresponding with entomologists in Europe, writing up a descriptive catalogue of his treasures. Such was the history of the man whom I had come to consult upon Jim's case without any definite hope. Simply to hear what he would have to say would have been a relief. I was very anxious, but I respected the intense, almost passionate, absorption with which he looked at a butterfly, as though on the bronze sheen of these frail wings, in the white tracings, in the gorgeous markings, he could see other things, an image of something as perishable and defying destruction as these delicate and lifeless tissues displaying a splendour unmarked by death.

"'Marvellous!' he repeated, looking up at me. 'Look! The beauty—but that is nothing—look at the accuracy, the harmony. And so fragile! And so strong! And so exact! This is Nature—the balance of colossal forces. Every star is so—and every blade of grass stands *so*—and the mighty Kosmos in perfect equilibrium produces—this. This wonder; this masterpiece of Nature—the great artist.'

# Literature Scale

**Reading Level 13-15**    It would have been in consonance with the spirit of Captain Vere should he on this occasion have concealed nothing from the condemned one; should he indeed have frankly disclosed to him the part he himself had played in bringing about the decision, at the same time revealing his actuated motives. On Billy's side it is not improbable that such a confession would have been received in much the same spirit that prompted it. Not without a sort of joy indeed he might have appreciated the brave opinion of him implied in his captain making such a confidant of him. Nor as to the sentence itself could he have been insensible that it was imparted to him as to one not afraid to die. Even more may have been. Captain Vere in the end may have developed the passion sometimes latent under an exterior stoical or indifferent. He was old enough to have been Billy's father. The austere devotee of military duty, letting himself melt back into what remains primeval in our formalised humanity, may in the end have caught Billy to his heart, even as Abraham may have caught young Isaac on the brink of resolutely offering him up in obedience to the exacting behest.

# Popular Fiction Scale

**Reading Level 1**

Morris the Moose wanted candy.
He went to the wrong store.
The man in the store said, "We don't sell candy. Can't you read?"
Then he showed Morris the candy store.
The man in the candy store said, "What would you like?"
Morris looked at the candy.
He liked the gumdrops.
He said, "Give me some of those."
The man said, "They are one for a penny. How much do you have?"
Morris looked. He had six pennies. "I have four pennies," he said.
The man laughed. "You have six! Can't you count? Don't you go to school?"
Morris asked, "What is school?"

**Reading Level 2**

Farley lived next door to Grover's garden. He looked out his window and watched Grover planting seeds. Farley called out:

"Hi, Grover! Can I help you plant those seeds?"

"Why certainly, little Farley! Do not forget to wear a sweater," said Grover. "It is just a little bit cold outside today."

Farley took out his favorite sweater. His grandmother had made it for him. Farley started to put on his sweater. Something was wrong! The hole in the top was too small for his head. The sleeves were too tight. The front of the sweater only came down to the middle of his stomach.

## Popular Fiction Scale

Reading Level 3

Andrew ran all the way home. Then he remembered he had to go to Mrs. Burrows' house to get the key. The secret recipe for freckle juice was folded carefully in the bottom of Andrew's shoe. He was going to put it inside his sock, but he was afraid if his foot got sweaty the ink might blur and he wouldn't be able to read it. So, inside his shoe was safe enough. Even if it was windy nothing could happen to it there. He made up his mind not to read it until he got home. He didn't want to waste any time getting there. And he wasn't the world's fastest reader anyway, even though he'd gotten better since last fall. Still, there might be some hard words that would take a while to figure out.

Reading Level 4

I knew there was no way out. Every kid at the swimming hole was watching as I started for the diving board. My legs trembled so much I could hardly walk. I was only eight years old and going to my death. I stopped as I reached the diving board. I looked down the river. All I had to do was run down the river bank and into the bushes. But if I did, I could never go home again. I was pretty young to go into the mountains and live like a naked savage. If I ran now, I would be a coward. Better by far to drown than to disgrace our family name.

I took a deep breath and ran right up the diving board and jumped into the swimming hole. This time I held my breath and kept my mouth shut as I paddled and kicked my way to the surface. Then I began paddling furiously with my arms and kicking my legs. The next thing I knew I had reached the river bank.

# Popular Fiction Scale

**Reading Level 5-6**      Our two coaches stopped at a kind of promontory where there was a collection of ruins and relics of the former cities. I had read up the history carefully the night before, but there was so much of it, and a lot of it was so gory and horrifying that I hoped our guests would not expect too much from me. As we started off in the direction of several broken Roman arches I was relieved to see that the people who were really interested in history had their own books with them and were already consulting them for what they wanted to see. Others gathered around the small shop which sold souvenirs and colour slides. Geoffrey joined me and we strolled toward the ruins.

"What a history this place has," he remarked. "One of the bloodiest on record, I'd say. I was reading it up coming over on the plane. Well, Christians in those days certainly suffered and died for their faith."

**Reading Level 7-8**      It was a sour and savage Korak who bade farewell to his baboon allies upon the following morning. They wished him to accompany them; but the ape-man had no heart for the society of any. Jungle life had encouraged taciturnity in him. His sorrow had deepened this to a sullen moroseness that could not brook even the savage companionship of the ill-natured baboons.

Brooding and despondent he took his solitary way into the deepest jungle. He moved along the ground when he knew that Numa was abroad and hungry. He took to the same trees that harbored Sheeta, the panther. He courted death in a hundred ways and a hundred forms. His mind was ever occupied with reminiscences of Meriem and the happy years that they had spent together. He realized now to the full what she had meant to him. The sweet face, the tanned, supple, little body, the bright smile that always had welcomed his return from the hunt haunted him continually.

# Popular Fiction Scale

Reading Level 9-10

"Consider, Captain. When we collided with the creature we were moving, according to the final readout, at warp-four, coming up to warp-six, which we never fully attained. If we suddenly fed a sustained burst of emergency power to the engines, the equivalent of warp-factor seven or eight, it is possible that the surfeit of energy—of food—would dangerously strain the creature's absorptive capacities.

"It would have two choices: to burst from overconsumption or abandon its hold on the *Enterprise*. If the former happens, we will at least be free to search for another jawanda, without our knowledge of its abilities and habits enlarged. If the latter, we may be able to engage the Boquian mechanism before the engorged creature can escape."

"It sounds good," admitted McCoy hopefully. "Why are the Lactrans leery of trying it?"

"Their reasons are twofold, Doctor. Should the jawanda *not* be overloaded by the surge of energy, we run the risk as stated by Engineer Scott of losing our warp-drive capability altogether. This would leave us with only impulse power on which to recross a considerable amount of space." His gaze momentarily checked a figure displayed on one of the science station's several screens.

# Life Sciences Scale

Reading Level 1

Have you ever visited a pond? The water is still. The air is quiet. You can hear a buzz.

Something is flying by. Splash! A shadow moves under the water. Many things are happening here.

A green frog is sitting on a green plant. Can you see it?

It is hard to see a frog when it sits still. How does the frog's color help it?

A frog can swim in the water. It can also hop on land.

Reading Level 2

Frogs and toads are amphibians without tails.

You can tell frogs apart by the pattern on their skins.

Some frogs have stripes.

The Swamp Tree frog has dark stripes down its back.

The Green Tree frog has a light stripe down each side and along its legs.

The Sheep frog has a light stripe down the middle of the back.

Which is which?

Sometimes size is a clue.

The Bullfrog is big. It can be 8 inches long. The Green frog is smaller. It gets to be only 3½ inches long.

# Life Sciences Scale

Reading Level 3          Most amphibians lay their eggs in the spring. Most of them lay their eggs in
water.

The female frog lays lots of eggs. Each one has a ball of jelly around it. The
eggs float in clumps on the water. The egg clumps are called spawn.

At first the eggs have no eyes or mouths. After a few days the eggs turn into
tadpoles. They hang onto plants with their suckers.

Soon gills grow on the tadpole's head. The tadpole breathes through these
gills and its skin while new gills grow inside its head. Then it loses the outside
gills.

Reading Level 4          Frogs, toads, and salamanders are *amphibians*. Amphibian comes from a Greek
word that means double life. Amphibians begin their life cycle as water animals.
They develop into air-breathing animals as they grow up.

Female amphibians lay their eggs in wet places. The eggs are covered with a
jelly-like material to protect them. The eggs hatch into larvae, or tadpoles. Tadpoles swim in the water and grow legs. When they are adults, amphibians live on
land and breathe air.

Toad tadpoles grow up quickly. It takes them only a few months to lose their
tails and become small toads. After that, it may take as long as three years for
them to become full-grown adults! Toads have been known to live to 30 to 40
years.

When frog eggs hatch into tadpoles it takes them a very long time to grow up.
Several years can go by before the tadpoles become frogs.

# Life Sciences Scale

Reading Level 5-6
Most land animals get all the oxygen they need by breathing with the lungs. They expand the rib cage with the chest muscles and draw air into the lungs.

The bullfrog, however, has three ways of getting oxygen. The first way is called "lung breathing." Because the frog does not have ribs, it must push air into its lungs with its mouth. About once or twice a minute, it draws in a mouthful of air, then closes its nostrils, and forces the air into the lungs. As it does you can see the frog twitch.

In addition to breathing with its lungs, the frog also absorbs oxygen through the roof of its mouth. The roof of the mouth has a network of tiny blood vessels that take in oxygen. To get oxygen to this network, the frog constantly draws air in and out of its mouth only. The process is called "mouth breathing."

Reading Level 7-8
While all this is happening, the embryo is getting longer. Now the tail bud begins to develop, and the embryo develops suckers beneath the place where the mouth will be. Although it is only about twenty-eight hours old and barely recognizable as a tadpole, the embryo now hatches. Toad embryos emerge very early, while frog and salamander embryos are further along when they come out of their jelly prisons. The small embryos hang by their suckers to the jelly. It will be five more hours before they can move their muscles at all.

When they are a little more than a day and a half old, their hearts begin to beat. Soon the blood begins to circulate through the gills, the developing eyes can be seen, the mouth opens, and the suckers begin to disappear. At two and a half days of age, when the blood starts circulating in the tail, they really look like tadpoles.

# Life Sciences Scale

**Reading Level 9-10**    When the tadpoles hatch, they have a tail, suckers and feathery external gills. Gradually, each tadpole undergoes a change of form, or metamorphosis. The external gills are replaced by internal gills. Then legs start to develop, the internal gills are replaced by lungs, and the tadpole becomes a small frog.

The eggs and tadpoles of frogs and toads are very vulnerable to predators, and some species have ingenious methods of protecting their young. Asian tree frogs lay their eggs in foams nests on leaves overhanging a stream or pool. When the eggs hatch, the tadpoles drop into the water below and continue their development there. The male smith frog builds a mud basin that fills with water and forms a private pool for the tadpoles. The tadpoles of some frogs develop in tiny pools of water that form in the leaves of certain plants.

The male midwife toad carries his string of eggs wrapped around his legs. When they are ready to hatch, he takes them to a pool of water. In some species, such as the Seychelles frog and the Surinam toad, the tadpoles are carried on the back of one of the parents until they have fully developed. The tadpoles of the mouth-breeding frog develop in the large vocal sac of the male.

**Reading Level 11-12**    Frogs and toads have an aquatic larval stage, the familiar tadpole. The fish-like tadpole has gills which are later lost in metamorphosis. The moist skin of frogs and other amphibians contains mucous glands that assist in maintaining the moisture. Moreover, the eggs of amphibians, laid in water or other moist areas, are usually covered with a gelatinous substance. Thus amphibians remain dependent on aquatic (or at least wet) environments in many ways.

This group also shows adaptations for living on land. Most importantly, adults have lungs adapted for air breathing and are therefore no longer dependent on water for gas exchange. (It can occur through the skin when amphibians are in water.) Furthermore, the two nostrils are connected to the mouth cavity to facilitate breathing through the lungs. Almost all amphibians have two pair of jointed appendages that permit locomotion both on land and in water. Frogs and toads also have sound-sensitive membranes ("external eardrums") on their bodies; such specialized sense organs are essential for land dwellers, because air does not transmit sound waves as efficiently as water. Finally, amphibians have a more efficient type of circulatory system than fish, including a heart with three chambers rather than two.

# Life Sciences Scale

Reading Level 13-15    The beginning of neurulation, or the formation of the nervous system in vertebrates, is marked by the appearance of a flattened plate of ectoderm that runs along the back of the embryo. Soon it reaches from the head to the tail. The outer surface of the cells seems to contract and the sides of the plate rise up, leaving a groove between the newly risen skin. Eventually, the skin that forms the neural ridges grows together, forming a hollow fluid-filled tube, the neural tube. As the organism becomes more and more mature, the front end of the neural tube grows and changes shape to form a brain, while the rest of the tube becomes the spinal nerve cord. Other parts of the nervous system form as outgrowths of the neural tube.

In the frog, the embryo becomes a self-supporting, free-swimming larva that initially is more fishlike than froglike. Later this larva, the tadpole, undergoes a metamorphosis in which its body is reshaped into a form that is somewhat more suitable for terrestrial life. The fishlike tail is reabsorbed, small fore- and hindlimbs form, and the organism begins to look more like an adult frog.

Reading Level 16+    It is possible to calculate that, if a frog oocyte (a developing egg cell) had the same number of ribosomal RNA genes as a body cell of the frog, it would take many years—far longer than a female frog lives—to make an egg with so many ribosomes.

Early in the development of the frog oocyte, however, the genes for ribosomal RNA undergo amplification: They are selectively replicated many hundredfold or thousandfold, while the rest of the nuclear DNA undergoes no further replication. These extra copies do not remain with the chromosome from which they are copied; they are "extrachromosomal" pieces of DNA that float free in the nucleus. They are all transcribed to yield ribosomal RNA, and egg development is completed in a matter of weeks instead of years. Amplification of ribosomal genes has been observed in other species. Amplification of nonribosomal genes—of structural genes coding for specific proteins, for example—has not yet been seen, despite intensive and critical search.

Rearrangement of structural genes has, however, been detected as a specific event in eukaryotic development. In the development of lymphocytes (the line of white blood cells that make antibodies in vertebrates), two genes that were originally located in different parts of the chromosome are physically combined to form a single functional structural gene that codes for one antibody polypeptide chain.

## Physical Sciences Scale

Reading Level 2

The earth we live on is in space. Space is all the room there is outside Earth's air. Earth—our home in space—is a planet.

A planet is a large world that travels around the sun. But the sun isn't a planet. It's a star that is a million times bigger than Earth.

Earth isn't the only planet that travels around the sun. There are eight others—some bigger than Earth, some smaller. The sun, together with its family of nine planets, is called the solar system.

Reading Level 3

The stars, like the sun, are always in the sky, and they are always shining. In the daytime the sky is so bright that the starts do not show. But when the sky darkens, there they are.

What are the stars, you wonder, and how do they twinkle?

Stars are huge balls of hot, hot gas. They are like the sun but they look small because they are much, much farther away. They are trillions and trillions of miles away, shining in black space, high above the air.

Space is empty and does not move. Stars do not twinkle there, but twinkling begins when starlight hits the air. The air moves and tosses the light around.

Reading Level 4

The Milky Way galaxy stretches across the sky in the shape of a large wheel. It has many millions of stars in it. Our sun is only one little star out near the edge of the galaxy. When the moon is not shining, the galaxy does not look milky. With a pair of binoculars, it is possible to see stars in the Milky Way.

Earth is a part of the Milky Way galaxy. To discover what our own galaxy is really like, scientists study other galaxies through powerful telescopes.

They know from these studies that galaxies turn and that stars circle around inside them. Planets may then circle around the stars, just as Earth revolves around its nearest star, the sun.

It is difficult to comprehend, or understand, how huge the Milky Way galaxy is. It is even more difficult to comprehend all the stars in it.

# Physical Sciences Scale

**Reading Level 5-6**

Black holes are probably the weirdest objects in space. They are created during a supernova explosion. If the collapsing core of the exploding star is large enough—more than four times the mass of our sun—it does not stop compressing when it gets as small as a neutron star. The matter crushes itself out of existence. All that remains is the gravity field—a black hole. The object is gone. Anything that comes close to it is swallowed up. Even a beam of light cannot escape.

Like vacuum cleaners in space, black holes suck up everything around them. But their reach is short. A black hole would have to be closer than one light-year to have even a small effect on the orbits of the planets in our solar system. A catastrophe such as the swallowing of the Earth or the sun is strictly science fiction.

**Reading Level 7-8**

As we have seen, a neutron star would be small and dense. It should also be rotating rapidly. All stars rotate, but most of them do so leisurely. For example, our Sun takes nearly one month to rotate once about its axis. A collapsing star speeds up as its size shrinks, just as an ice skater during a pirouette speeds up when she pulls in her arms. This phenomenon is a direct consequence of a law of physics known as the conservation of angular momentum, which holds that the total amount of angular momentum in a system remains constant. An ordinary star rotating once a month would be spinning faster than once a second if compressed to the size of a neutron star.

In addition to having rapid rotation, we expect a neutron star to have an intense magnetic field. It is probably safe to say that every star has a magnetic field of some strength.

## Physical Sciences Scale

Reading Level 9-10        William Herschel (1738-1822) and his sister, Caroline Herschel (1750-1848), carefully observed many binary star systems. They thought that many pairs of stars were associated with each other by gravitational forces that made them move in orbits around a common point. When they saw these orbital motions, they proved that Newton's law of gravitation operates outside our own solar system.

Most stars in our galaxy shine steadily, but more than 20,000 stars are called variables because their light output changes. Over half are pulsating variable stars that change periodically in size and brightness. Red variables take months or years between their brightest and faintest periods. It is interesting to observe the famous variable red supergiant Mira in Cetus. Because Mira changes from its maximum bright red to invisible, it was nicknamed "The Wonderful." Shorter period stars, such as the Cepheid variables, are less common but are important because their light output is used to measure distances in space. You can see the first known Cepheid variable, delta Cephei. It was discovered in 1784 by the teenage English astronomer John Goodricke two years before he died at the age of 21.

Reading Level 11-12        In this way, a general explanation of the different types of galaxies begins to emerge. In an elliptical galaxy, the stars all formed before the gas had time to flatten into a disk; the more spheroidal the galaxy, the more rapidly this formation occurred. In a spiral galaxy, the stars of population II formed before the end of the flattening phase. When the gas was concentrated in the shape of a flat disk, the stars formed from the gas where the gas was located—i.e., in the disk. It remains to be explained why the formation of stars took place more rapidly in the elliptical than in the spiral galaxies. Inasmuch as we cannot explain in detail how stars form, it is not easy to answer that question. It seems that the rate of formation of stars is related to the density of the gas; the denser the gas, the faster the rate of formation of stars. Therefore, some people have believed that the density of the gas making up the protogalaxy was higher in elliptical galaxies than in spiral galaxies. However, when we consider the average density of matter, currently in the form of stars, that is contained in a galaxy, that average density does not seem to be significantly higher in the ellipticals.

# Physical Sciences Scale

Reading Level 13-15    To understand how we can have inflation, let us note that Einstein's general theory of relativity tells us that the rate of the universe's expansion is directly related to the density of matter and radiation in it, and since mass and energy are equivalent ($E=mc^2$), this means that the universe's expansion is related to energy density; the higher the universe's energy density, the higher its rate of expansion; and conversely, the lower the energy density, the lower the rate of expansion. Because the early universe was very dense, it initially expanded very rapidly. (It had to or it wouldn't have expanded at all.) In the standard model for cosmological expansion, as time went on, the density decreased, and so the rate of expansion decreased. The reason that the density decreases is that the expansion adds space, so the mass energy is spread out over a larger and larger volume of space. The decrease in the energy density decreases the rate of expansion yet further. But the universe could inflate at a constant rate if somehow the density remained constant, so that even though the distance scale gets bigger, the amount of energy per unit volume remains the same.

Reading Level 16+    Since the invention of GUTs in 1974, particle theorists have been vigorously working on attempts to construct the ultimate theory of nature—an elegant theory which would include a quantum description of gravity. The characteristic energy scale of such a theory is presumably the Planck scale, $10^{19}$GeV, a point at which the gravitational interactions of elementary particles become comparable in strength to the other types of interactions. It is then hoped that a GUT would emerge as a low-energy approximation.

The latest and most successful of these attempts at unification is a radically new kind of particle theory known as 'superstring theory.' Superstrings represent a dramatic departure from conventional theories in that particles are viewed as ultramicroscopic strings (length = $10^{-33}$ centimeters). Furthermore, according to this theory, the universe has *nine* spatial dimensions. Early in the history of the universe, when the temperature cooled below $10^{32}$ degrees Kelvin, all spatial dimensions, except the three we know today, stopped expanding and remained curled up with an unobservably small extent. As bizarre as the theory may sound, the superstring theory has been shown to possess a number of unique properties crucial to a quantum theory of gravity, and it has totally captured the attention of a large fraction of the worldwide particle theory community.

# Narrative Social Studies Scale

**Reading Level 1**

A horse clattered into the barnyard.

"It's Father!" Debby cried.

Before anyone could get to the door, Father was in the kitchen. Everyone was talking at once.

"Let Father talk," said Mother.

Father told them that the British were coming for the guns stored in Concord. "We believe," he said, "that they will march tonight. But when they get to Concord, they will find nothing there. We have moved the guns out. We have stored them in new hiding places in other villages. We have worked very hard."

Grandmother was frightened. "Then they will come up Lexington Road!" she said. "Quick! Put on your coats, children!"

---

**Reading Level 2**

"Send Charles Darragh to me at once."

John sat stiffly in front of the uniformed man. It seemed like a year before Charles arrived.

"Why, John," Charles said in surprise.

John smiled. Now he could prove that he spied for General Washington. "Mother sent me. I have some messages for General Washington."

John took the loose button from his pocket. "There is a message in Father's code hidden inside."

Charles uncovered the button. He took out the message and looked at it.

"Please decode the message right away," the tall man said.

"Don't, Charles," said John. "Only General Washington is supposed to know."

Charles laughed at his brother. "John, this is General Washington."

# Narrative Social Studies Scale

**Reading Level 3**

Phoebe's mind was whirling as she hurried back toward the house. She was frightened, but she was also determined. She would save General Washington! She had long ago figured that he would likely be shot. During dinner he always sat in a chair by the window. He would make an easy target for anyone sitting outside.

If only she could get him to change his place, away from that window! His good friend General Gates would be a dinner guest at the house this evening. Everyone else was part of the family or a member of the bodyguard. Over and over she said their names. No one's name began with T.

**Reading Level 4**

It was in the morning when Jonathan first heard the bell. He was standing in the warm, open field feeling hot, dirty and bored. His father, not far off, limped as he worked along the newly turned rows of corn. As for Jonathan, he was day-dreaming, daydreaming about being a soldier.

His older brother was a soldier with General Washington in Pennsylvania. His cousin had joined a county regiment. Jonathan kept waiting for his father to say that he, too, could join. He was, after all, thirteen. But his father only put him off.

Jonathan dreamed of one day taking up a gun himself and fighting the enemy. For he had heard his father and his father's friends talk many times about the tyrannical British; their cruel mercenary allies, the German-speaking Hessians; and the hated Tories, those American traitors who had sided with the brutal English king.

# Narrative Social Studies Scale

Reading Level 5-6          Standing quietly in the crowd, he saw Sam Adams, pretending to be a most innocent bystander. It looked to Johnny as if the dog fox had eaten a couple of fat pullets, and had a third in his mouth.

As they started marching back to the center of town, they passed the Coffin House at the head of Griffin's Wharf. A window opened.

"Well, boys," said a voice, so cold one hardly knew whether he spoke in anger or not, "you've had a fine night for your Indian caper, haven't you? But mind... you've got to pay the fiddler yet."

It was the British Admiral Montague.

"Come on down here," someone yelled, "and we'll settle that score tonight."

The Admiral pulled in his head and slapped down the window.

Johnny and Rab knew, and men like the Observers knew, but the best of all Sam Adams knew, that the fiddler would have to be paid.

Reading Level 7-8          General Thomas Gage awoke before dawn one morning early in April 1775 and went to his office in Province House overlooking Boston Harbor. He paced back and forth, his hands clasped behind his back, deep in thought.

There was a lot to think about. On the desk lay reports from spies, "good" Yankees loyal to their king. Their reports detailed, among other things, the movements of John Hancock and Sam Adams. Both were preparing to attend the Second Continental Congress and would be staying with Hancock's relative, the Reverend Jonas Clark, at Lexington, a village twelve miles northwest of Boston. Five miles up the road, at Concord, patriots had stored enough supplies for a small army: muskets and cannon, barrels of gunpowder and bullets, tents, medicines, food, entrenching tools.

Gage made his plans carefully, telling as few people as possible of his intentions. On the eighteenth of April, Redcoats would be rowed across Boston Harbor under cover of darkness for a raid to capture the patriot leaders and destroy their supplies. With one swift blow Gage would smash the rebellion before it began.

# Narrative Social Studies Scale

**Reading Level 9-10**

In July, through the offices of a friend (Dolly), I received a letter from John Hancock, now president of the Continental Congress, recommending my cousin Matthias Ogden and me to the attention of the recently appointed commanding general of the Continental Army, George Washington of Virginia.

I ought to mention that Dolly was appalled when news came to us that Washington had been chosen. "John was supposed to command the army. I don't understand it."

But then, at the time, no one understood how Washington and his Virginia confederates had managed to wrest for themselves the leadership of what was essentially a New England array. Working together in perfect concert and displaying at all times the most exquisite loyalty to one another, the Virginians pushed to one side not only John Hancock but such talented commanders as Gates and Lee and Artemus Ward. As a matter of course, John Adams would betray his fellow New Englander John Hancock. Lacking personal loyalty to one another as well as any true policy, the New Englanders and the New Yorkers from the beginning gave over to the Virginia junto the American republic—and with relish the junto proceeded to rule us for the better part of a half-century.

**Reading Level 11-12**

The missive was dated "Thursday evening, 9 o'clock, Nov. 4, 1773." The Loyal Nine had collaborated on the text, as usual, and perhaps the vengeful tone reflected the lingering sting of cuts and bruises suffered in the fracas at Clark's warehouse.

The tea consignees, despite what appeared to be overwhelming odds, didn't scare easily. If anything, their resistance stiffened.

Earlier on Thursday, the selectmen of Boston had issued a notice to the community to attend a special town meeting and next day to discuss this alarming affair. The selectmen had been persuaded to convene the townspeople to give formal expression to the community's sentiments regarding the tea, especially since one of the consignees, and several of their friends, so the Gazette reported, had let it be known that if the harassed gentlemen were asked properly, and not brutishly, they would indeed resign—a report evidently without substance.

On Thursday, also, Governor Hutchinson summoned his Council, the small, select upper body of the Provincial legislature, to meet with him to determine an official course of action. Hutchinson had no delusions regarding the degree of support he might expect from his Council, the members of which he knew to be predominantly anti-administration, but he felt that it was his duty to make the try.

## Expository Social Studies Scale

Reading Level 2     At first there was the Pilgrim family.

Then more people came to this country. There were other bigger families.

These families were called COLONIES. There were thirteen colonies at one time.

Thirteen families.

Sometimes they did not get along together.

They quarreled.

The leaders thought the thirteen groups should live together as one family. How could this be done? What would hold the people together?

One day the leaders met in Philadelphia.

They came by boat, by horseback, by stagecoach, and on foot.

They wrote the CONSTITUTION.

Reading Level 3     When the British were coming to Philadelphia, the Liberty Bell was taken down from its tower. It was hidden under the floor of a church so that no enemy soldiers could find it.

The Congress had to move from Philadelphia to another city—and another—and another. Always, the Declaration of Independence went with them. The Declaration was taken to many different places. Once it even spent the night in a barn.

It was a dark and sad time for the United States of America. But some of the countries across the sea in Europe sent help.

Reading Level 4     When the Revolutionary War started in 1776, Americans fought under many different flags. One flag had a pine tree on it and the words "An Appeal to Heaven." Another had a rattlesnake and the words "Don't Tread On Me." Others had "Liberty or Death" or "Conquer or Die."

The new flag had thirteen stripes—seven red and six white—and thirteen white stars on a field of blue. No one knows who designed this flag or made the first one.

According to one story, the first flag was made by Betsy Ross. It is true that Betsy Ross did sew flags during the Revolutionary War. And she lived in Philadelphia. Her house is now a national shrine. But there is no proof that she made the first official American flag.

# Expository Social Studies Scale

**Reading Level 5-6**     During the nearly two centuries of British rule, the colonists' attitude toward England gradually changed. The early colonists had regarded themselves as English people who happened to live across the ocean from their mother country. For the most part they had been content to be ruled by lawmakers and governors sent from England. The children and grandchildren of these early colonists wanted more of a say in their government, and so England had allowed them to elect assemblies with limited powers. By the 1760s, this was not enough for many colonists. A few were even in favor of the colonies separating from England and becoming a new country.

There were several reasons for these growing feelings. By the mid-1700s, the colonies were home to many thousands of less-wealthy English people and to thousands more who had come from such countries as Ireland, Scotland, Germany, the Netherlands, France, and Sweden. Most of these people had never been to Great Britain, did little or no business with the British, and felt little loyalty to England.

**Reading Level 7-8**     The London merchants began to worry. To save themselves, they demanded that Parliament repeal the Stamp Act. Benjamin Franklin, representing the colonies in London, went to the House of Commons and warned the British that they were on the road to ruin. If they did not change their policies, there would very likely be rebellion. The Americans, he explained, dearly loved their Mother England, but they loved their liberties even more.

The rulers of Britain might still have saved the situation. If they had known the colonists better, they would have realized that Americans would not let their lives be run by others. A shrewder British government might have worked out a cooperative empire. Then there might never have been a War of Independence. But the rulers of Britain were near-sighted and short-sighted. They thought that government by Parliament had to be all-or-nothing. Unlike the Americans, they were not willing to compromise.

# Expository Social Studies Scale

Reading Level 9-10    Americans who were loyal to Britain during the Revolutionary War were called Tories, or Loyalists. They supported the right of Britain to rule the Colonies. This does not mean that they approved of the Crown's treatment of the Colonies. Many, like the rebel patriots, were for individual liberties and against taxation without representation. But the Loyalists recognized the king's ultimate authority in America.

About five hundred thousand Americans (fifteen to thirty-six percent of the white population) remained loyal to Britain between 1775 and 1783. In 1780, John Adams believed that five percent of Americans were loyal, but he revised his estimate in 1815 as he reflected on the struggle for independence. He concluded that about one-third of the people opposed the Revolution. Loyalism was weakest in the oldest, best-established colonies, such as Connecticut and Virginia. But although Loyalists were a minority in every colony, there were enough of them to forestall an American victory.

Colonists chose Loyalism for many reasons. Although there were exceptions, most Loyalists were landowners, professionals, or government officials, and many were wealthy. In many cases they remained loyal in an attempt to preserve their standing in the community.

Reading Level 11-12    Events like Lexington and Concord, followed by the larger battle at Breed's Hill, cut sharply through the strata of American society. Many men who previously had accepted things as they were now had to declare themselves for or against independence. Conservatives and, in general, those who held offices in America struggled to maintain the connection with England. They angered those who regarded war as the only course, and with each violent incident the breach widened. Radical leaders like Sam Adams, who had urged independence for nearly a decade, seized upon the division and fanned the flames of revolution to white heat. Another firebrand, Thomas Paine, published his pamphlet *Common Sense*, and at once it became a best seller. The propagandist, as always, had put into words what many men had been thinking but could not say.

The British seemed continually to provide reasons for colonial charges against them. The king had already announced that blows must decide the issue, and when he received what was called the Olive Branch Petition from the colonies, he rejected it, stigmatizing all Americans as disloyal. The moderate William Pitt proposed a compromise, but Parliament rejected it.

# Expository Social Studies Scale

**Reading Level 13-15**     Beginning in 1740, a series of crises undermined the stability of these established political and social orders. Religious turmoil, war with France, and an economic cycle of boom and bust struck in rapid succession. Britain's sudden imposition of new measures of taxation and control prompted riots, petitions, and the movement for American independence. By 1775, many colonists had repudiated British rule and the traditional monarchical system of government. Many other Americans actively questioned the authority of existing religious institutions and the legitimacy of established political and social distinctions. The struggle for home rule raised the crucial question of who should rule at home.

Between 1776 and 1820, the citizens of the new United States created a republican institutional order. While fighting a financially draining war against Great Britain, they devised effective state constitutions and governments. Subsequently, they organized themselves into a strong national union and began the expansion into the trans-Appalachian west. Americans debated, argued, and even fought bitterly with one another during these years. They were divided into distinct social groups, each seeking to defend or extend its own values and interests.

In the end, the American Revolution had both radical and conservative results.

**Reading Level 16+**     What does lie at the core of the consensus that sustains the Congress, the Philadelphia Convention, the Federalist, and we must add now, the first Congress? It is, he insists, an agreed-upon public philosophy, stated in propositional form (e.g., but only e.g., all men are created equal), and propositional in both of the two senses of that ambiguous word "proposition": that of a truth that is asserted (as self-evident, as demonstrated, or as demonstrable); and that of an intention to be realized, an operation to be performed (as when we say: I propose to, etc.)—that, then, on the one hand, of a doctrine, and that, on the other, of a project, but claiming assent on grounds of reason. He will attempt, as he proceeds, to identify the content of the proposition; but sound methodology, as he understands it, requires that we should first be clear as to the kind of proposition it is and the kind of proposition it is not, and his theses here are, as I believe, theses of the first importance for the contemporary conservative movement, if it is to relate itself correctly to the origins of the tradition that it purports to cherish.

# Part III
# Discussion and Analysis
# of Scaled Passages

# CHAPTER 5

# The Literature and Popular Fiction Scales

## The Literature Scale

The literature passages on pp. 20-24 were taken from works of narrative fiction, the most widely read form of literature. Most passages are from novels or book-length works; one is from a short story. Passages at the beginning of the scale are from children's literature; the higher level passages are from established works of adult literature. Children's literature is seen as part of a literary continuum, not as a separate genre.[1] The set of scaled literature passages thus reflects, however abbreviatedly and incompletely, the range of good narrative fiction and the development of complexity within it. See Appendix C, "Bibliographic Information on the Literature Scale," p. 98, for full references.

### Progression of Difficulty

At the easiest reading levels (1 and 2), books of narrative fiction for children are structurally simple, usually centering on one main character and one plot thread with events presented in chronological order. The illustrations may help children follow the story by depicting incidents (as in *The Bears on Hemlock Mountain*, from which passage 2, p. 20, is taken) or even by depicting the entire tale.

The total number of different words in stories at these reading levels is small. *Green Eggs and Ham*, by Dr. Seuss, from which passage 1 (p. 20) is taken, is a virtuoso

---

[1] This position is supported by the editors of *Only Connect: Readings in Children's Literature* (Egoff, Stubbs, & Ashley, 1969): "Our primary aim has been to find selections that deal with children's literature as an essential part of the whole realm of literary activity, to be discussed in the same terms and judged by the same standards that would apply to any other branch of writing. We do not subscribe to the view that the criticism of children's books calls for the adoption of a special scale of values." More recent scholarship on children's literature continues to maintain this position, e.g.: "In many ways, the literary criteria that apply to adult books and children's books are the same. The best books have that most elusive component, a distinctive literary style. A well-constructed plot; sound characterization with no stereotypes; dialogue that flows naturally and is appropriate to the speaker's age, education, and milieu; and a pervasive theme are equally important in children's and adults' fiction" (Sutherland, 1980, p. vii). Confirmation of this continuity does not close the gap between the teaching of reading, with its associated reading research, and the teaching of literature, with its associated literary theory (see Bodgan & Straw, 1990).

example of variations on a fifty-word vocabulary. Words, sentences, and actions are frequently repeated, building up familiar patterns that help the beginning reader anticipate language and events.

Characteristically, literature on the next reading levels (3 and 4) is substantially lengthier, with plots now multiple-stranded and events sometimes shifted out of chronological order. Such increased structural complexity is evident in Roald Dahl's *The Magic Finger*, the source of passage 3 (p. 21). Characters, too, are generally more complicated and more subtle as well as more numerous. The language at reading levels 3 and 4 shows a great expansion in vocabulary over the language of literature at the first two levels; sentence structures, too, are more varied and intricate, bearing more information and stating more relationships. Compare the simple contrast expressed in passage 2: "There were no bears. But up the path came his father, carrying his gun." with this contrast from passage 4: "I was too frightened to hang on much longer, yet frightened even more to let loose." At levels 3 and 4, language may be used figuratively as well as literally, as in "We felt like we'd stolen the moon" from passage 4. Thus, as we move up the literature scale, the knowledge of language needed by the reader increases both in scope and depth.

By at least reading level 5-6, literature makes strong demands on experiential understanding—personal experiences not only undergone but reflected upon—and on a reader's imaginative ability to encompass experiences different from his or her own. The thoughts and feelings of characters are more fully revealed, and substantial issues are more explicitly explored, as illustrated in reading level 5-6, from *The Light in the Forest*, and reading level 7-8, from *The Call of the Wild* (p. 22).

Linguistic and experiential demands do not always increase in tandem. For example, Conrad's language in the 11-12th reading level passage (p. 23) does not seem more difficult than the language of reading level 9-10, from Poe. But experientially and intellectually, a reader must bring more to bear to understand the symbolic meaning of the butterfly and the implications about man—especially as these function to comment on events and characters in *Lord Jim*—than to understand the extreme but narrow experience of Poe's single focal character. Much more must be inferred by the reader of Conrad's passage than by the reader of Poe's.

Literature at reading level 9-10 and beyond makes powerful linguistic, experiential, and intellectual demands of a reader. Intellectually, a reader must not only (a) be able to grasp the often profound issues authors explore through their narratives but (b) bring to the interpretation of those narratives a wide literary and cultural knowledge. The passage from *Billy Budd* at reading level 13-15 illustrates such intellectual demands. Sentence structures such as "Nor as to the sentence itself could he have been insensible that it was imparted to him as to one not afraid to die," and language such as *actuated* and the particular meaning here of *brave*, are not generally familiar. Understanding the Biblical reference to Abraham's willingness to sacrifice his son is essential to receiving, both conceptually and emotionally, the import of the moment Melville describes. Furthermore, the passage does not describe events as actually occurring but as possibilities for the reader to contemplate. The details of the suggested scene must be filled in by the reader's imagination, informed by an understanding of the characters.

In academic contexts, a reader is increasingly expected to apply techniques of literary criticism in order to analyze how a work of literature is constructed and to delineate its meanings. Thus, reading at the upper levels of the literature scale may require both the skills of a literary specialist and the general knowledge of an educated reader. Literary works from earlier centuries and different cultures make particular demands on this broad knowledge. Aesthetic considerations as well as historical changes in style and vocabulary create language structures that diverge significantly from contemporary, everyday usage. The absence of a literature passage at the 16+ reading level does not reflect a belief that literature fails to offer reading as challenging as that at the top of the expository history or the science scales. While James Joyce's *Finnegan's Wake* provided a passage we could have positioned at reading level 16+, we decided against using it because it seemed too unique to be generally useful.

Literature is seen, through this series of scaled passages, as increasing in difficulty along several dimensions: linguistic, structural, experiential and intellectual. The reading level of literature texts at the upper end of the scale may be underestimated by those traditional readability measures that focus on sentence length and unfamiliar vocabulary. The language of literature—in contrast especially to the language of science—does not contain a technical vocabulary. Sentence length and complexity are reduced by dialogue and the occasional use of short, simple sentences for effect. Using measures of linguistic features, then, may not fully reflect the difficulty of literature at the upper levels where meanings—in contrast to the meanings of informational reading—are dramatized rather than stated, and exist on more than a literal reading level.

## Criteria and Benchmarks

In assessing the difficulty levels of the literature passages, we asked ourselves, "What does the reader need to bring to the text in order to understand it?" Specifically: "How wide a vocabulary? Familiarity with what kinds of sentence structures? Life experiences of what depth and breadth? How much skill and sophistication in literary analysis? How much cultural and literary knowledge?" Using these criteria, we established benchmarks for groupings of scaled levels. (See Table 5-1, p. 52.)

### 1. How wide a vocabulary is needed?

- *At reading levels 1 and 2:* mainly short, familiar words.
- *At reading levels 3, 4 and 5-6:* a much more varied vocabulary but still generally familiar words, and some awareness of figurative language.
- *At reading levels 7-8 through 11-12:* an increasing number of uncommon words and awareness of non-literal meanings.
- *At college and graduate reading levels:* a wide vocabulary and sensitivity to levels of meaning.

### 2. Familiarity with what kinds of sentence structures?

- *At reading levels 1 and 2:* short, simply constructed sentences for the most part, and sentences reiterating a pattern.
- *At reading levels 3 and 4:* more elaborated and complex sentences that combine more information and assert more relationships among ideas.
- *At reading levels 5-6 and 7-8:* sentences significantly more formal than everyday language.
- *At reading levels 9-10 and beyond:* complex and formal sentence structures. For reading literature of earlier historical periods, sentences structured in currently uncommon patterns. Familiarity with such language is attained through

**Table 5-1**
What the Reader Needs to Bring to the Text to Read **Literature** with Understanding

| Reading Levels | 1 | 2 | 3 | 4 | 5–6 | 7–8 | 9–10 | 11–12 | 13–15 (College) |
|---|---|---|---|---|---|---|---|---|---|
| **Knowledge of vocabulary** | Mainly familiar words, often repeated. | | More varied, but generally familiar; some figurative language. | | | Increasing number of uncommon words; non-literal meanings. | | | Wide vocabulary and range of meaning levels. |
| **Familiarity with sentence structures** | Mainly short and simply constructed; patterns often reiterated. | | More elaborated and complex; more information included and more relationships and ideas asserted. | | Significantly more formal than everyday language. | | Often complex and formal; currently uncommon structures appear in literature of earlier periods. | | |
| **Depth and breadth of life experiences** | Common experiences with family and community. Capacity for imaginative identification with animals and fantasy figures. | | | | Capacity for complex emotions and judgments, for reflection, for imaginative grasp of the inner lives of others. Especially at the higher levels of this range, the capacity to entertain unusual perspectives and multiple values. | | | | |
| **Cultural and literary knowledge** | General background knowledge. | | | | | | | | Cultural and literary knowledge increasingly essential for understanding literature, especially from other periods and cultures. |
| **Skill in literary analysis** | A sense of story and familiarity with story conventions. | | | In school settings, ability to identify and think about elements of fiction such as character, plot, and setting. | | | Literary analysis increasingly required for interpreting literature in academic contexts. | | |

a wide reading of literature.

3. **Life experiences of what depth and breadth?**

   *By reading level 5 and beyond,* experiences evoking complex emotions and reflective responses gain importance. Especially for the higher levels of this range, uncommon experiences, unusual perspectives and multiple values must be appreciated.

4. **How much cultural and literary knowledge?**

   *By reading levels 11-12 through 16+ (college graduate),* such knowledge is essential for understanding literature, especially works from other periods and cultures.

5. **How much skill and sophistication in literary analysis?**

   *At reading levels 11-12 through college graduate level,* knowledge of and skill in literary analysis are generally required for interpreting literature in academic contexts.

## Development of the Scale

The search for suitable material for the literature scale started at its extremes, with Dr. Seuss chosen as the author of the easiest passage and Herman Melville chosen as the source of the hardest. Of the many Dr. Seuss books, *Green Eggs and Ham* was selected for its simplicity of language (a vocabulary of only 50 short, high frequency, mostly regularly spelled words) and for its demonstration that repetition need not mean monotony—in addition, of course, to its literary qualities. The passage selected from Herman Melville was the most difficult in the set in terms of sentence structure, vocabulary, references, and proportion of implication to assertion. The James Joyce passage we considered but finally discarded for reading level 16+ approached poetry in the ambiguity and compression of its language, asking to be read more like poetry than prose, with deliberate consideration of each word. To understand what Joyce is doing with language in *Finnegan's Wake,* readers need an encyclopedic store of information and knowledge of languages other than modern English. Because Joyce violated conventions of language and of literary form, readers cannot rely on familiarity with these conventions, but must construct meanings unconventionally as they read.

Filling in the intervening steps on the scale required examining much literature and discarding many potential passages. Some of the problems of devising this scale became apparent as we looked closely at *Winnie-the-Pooh,* deciding finally not to use a passage from it. An analysis of several passages from the book revealed its wide variations in sophistication of language and content. The style ranged from short, simple sentences like "Have you seen Pooh?" to Owl's pedantic language: "However, the prospects are rapidly becoming more favorable," and a 196-word sentence conveying the effect of his long-windedness. Such variations, which are part of the charm and appeal of Milne's style, raised questions about the level of comprehension expected of young readers. Did they need to be familiar with Owl's vocabulary and able to follow that long sentence, or only be able to experience the effect of stuffy language and interminable syntax? Children too young to read the book could appreciate the effects; children with the linguistic experience to comprehend all the words and sentences might be too old to want to read the book. *Winnie-the-Pooh* seemed more a book for parents to read aloud to their children—a book that parents would *enjoy* reading aloud, with adult meanings as well as child meanings. It was a book that served to confront us with the variations in style and the layers of meaning characteristic of good literature.

A more modern classic for older readers, *Catcher in the Rye*, was also eliminated as a passage source because of the considerable discrepancy between its language (some samples scored at a 4th or 5-6th reading level by the new Dale-Chall formula) and the more mature experiential level needed for comprehending the book.

While the general location of passages on the scale was evident as they were being selected, distinctions between adjacent levels became sharpened only as a number of passages were considered together and compared. Making clear distinctions between adjacent passages at reading levels 5-6 through 11-12 was particularly challenging.

# The Popular Fiction Scale

The Popular Fiction Scale on pp. 25-28 was constructed after it became clear that the literature scale was not an entirely appropriate guide for judging the reading level of popular works. The passages of the popular fiction scale were selected to represent a variety of popular fiction forms and styles in books (often published in series) and magazines—romances, adventure stories, and science fiction—intended for audiences of different ages: children, young people, and adults.

The Popular Fiction Scale has only seven levels, in contrast to nine levels for literature. By its very nature of being accessible to a large audience, popular fiction does not reach the high levels of difficulty that literature does. Generally, the popular fiction selections, even those at the highest levels, do not require sophisticated literary analysis, broad cultural background, or a capacity for reflecting on a range of experiences and a multiplicity of values—demands made on readers by the highest-level passages in the literature scale. Neither do the historical and cross-cultural dimensions of those passages carry over to popular fiction, which is essentially contemporary. The reading level of popular fiction varies more directly in proportion to its linguistic difficulty (vocabulary and sentence structure) than is true for the literature selections. Thus it is more accurately measured by most traditional readability formulas, which quantify such linguistic features.[2]

## Progression of Difficulty

Passages at the first three levels in the popular fiction scale show many of the same characteristics of increasing difficulty as do those in the literature scale. The language and content of the first two passages are simple and redundant. Sentences are short; vocabulary is common and repeated often. Characters are few, and plots focus on a single line of development. Linguistic complexity, especially in terms of sentence structure, increases in passage 3. A wider array of characters and situations is portrayed in the short novel from which the passage at reading level 3 was taken, and the plot development is more complicated. In all of the popular fiction passages at these

---

[2] It should be noted that the New Dale-Chall Readability Formula measures the semantic and syntactic features as well as several qualitative aspects used for the scales.

three reading levels, meanings are direct and explicit, in contrast to the literary passages which contained some implication as early as the second reading level.

While the passage at reading level 4 still employs short sentences that make a single point, one or two require something beyond literal understanding (e.g., "I was only eight years old and going to my death"). The passage makes more demands of the reader than the previous passage in terms of vocabulary and conceptual understanding. It portrays a familiar situation but one that involves some emotional complexity. The most difficult words (*martyr, disgrace*) are important for understanding the passage.

Passages at reading levels 5-6 through 9-10 are markedly more difficult in their language. Comprehension of the 5-6 reading level passage does not, however, require understanding all of the relatively sophisticated vocabulary. While its setting is unfamiliar, its emotional content is quite common. Redundancy and conformity to conventional expectations make this passage somewhat easier reading than a measure of its vocabulary and sentence length indicates.

The advanced vocabulary of the 7-8th reading level passage seems more essential to conveying its meaning: the portrayal of a severe emotional state, with which a reader might not identify as readily as with the emotions portrayed in the previous three passages. This selection focuses on a state of mind rather than on actions or dialogue, which are often easier to grasp.

The linguistic and conceptual demands on the reader increase again for the 9-10th reading level passage. The most challenging aspect of this passage is its vocabulary, whose difficulty has two dimensions: words that are highly sophisticated and uncommon in the English language (*surfeit, engorged*) and words that are science-fiction related (*warp-factor, readout*). The science-related language of the passage was judged to be relatively more familiar to readers today than the infrequent, sophisticated words; because the passage's redundancy renders familiarity with every word unnecessary and because readers would probably already know some of the science-fiction terms through television and movies, it was placed on a 9-10th reading level. The passage is conceptually complex in terms of the multiple choices and consequences that it juggles, requiring the reader to follow a pattern of logical reasoning. It makes further demands on the reader in terms of assuming some background knowledge of the conventions and technical accoutrements of the universe of science fiction.

## Criteria and Benchmarks

In assessing the difficulty levels of the popular fiction passages, we asked, "What does the reader need to bring to the text in order to understand it?" Specifically: "How wide a vocabulary? Familiarity with what kinds of sentence structures? Life experiences of what depth and breadth?" These same criteria were used in assessing the difficulty of the literature scale. The final two criteria for the literature passages—skill and sophistication in literary analysis, and cultural and literary knowledge—were not generally relevant to popular fiction because of its nature and the less academic contexts in which it is commonly read. Instead, we asked what prior reading experiences might be helpful for the reader. Using these criteria, we established benchmarks for groupings of scaled levels. (See Table 5-2, p. 56.)

### 1. How wide a vocabulary is needed?

- *At reading levels 1 through 3*: mainly short, familiar words, frequently repeated;

**Table 5-2**
What the Reader Needs to Bring to the Text to Read **Popular Fiction** with Understanding

| Reading Levels | 1 | 2 | 3 | 4 | 5-6 | 7-8 | 9-10 |
|---|---|---|---|---|---|---|---|
| **Knowledge of vocabulary** | Mainly familiar words, frequently repeated; literal meanings. | | | Awareness of non-literal meanings. | A wider range of general vocabulary; for some texts, particularly science-fiction, some current specialized terms. | | |
| **Familiarity with sentence structures** | Mainly short and simply constructed. | | Somewhat more complex but not dense with information. | | Increasingly more lengthy, complex and dense than everyday speech. | | |
| **Depth and breadth of life experiences** | Common experiences around family and community. | | | | Wider contacts with the world and a broader range of experiences. | | |
| **Cultural and literary knowledge** | A sense of story and a background of general knowledge. | | | | Familiarity with the conventions of particular genres facilitates reading. | | |

literal meanings.

- *At reading level 4*: awareness of non-literal meanings begins to be needed.
- *At reading levels 5-6 through 9-10*: a wider range of general vocabulary, and for some texts, particularly science-fiction, some current specialized terms. Redundancy of texts may reduce the need for familiarity with every word.

2. **Familiarity with what kinds of sentence structures?**
- *At reading levels 1 and 2*: mainly short and simply constructed sentences.
- *At reading levels 3 and 4*: somewhat more complex and varied sentences, but not heavily loaded with information.
- *At reading levels 5-6 through 9-10*: sentences increasingly more lengthy, complex and dense than in everyday speech.

3. **Life experiences of what depth and breadth?**
   *By reading level 5-6 and beyond*: wider contacts with the external world and a broader range of experiences. No unusual capacity for reflectiveness, complex judgments, or grasping the inner lives of characters seems required.

4. **What prior reading experiences?**
- *By reading level 5-6*: a background of general knowledge.
- *At reading levels 7-8 and 9-10*: familiarity with the conventions of a particular genre, such as murder mysteries and science fiction, may facilitate reading but is not essential.

## Comparison of the Popular Fiction and Literature Scales

Qualitative differences between the demands that literature and popular fiction make on readers may be seen by comparing two passages, one from each scale, at the same reading level. Since more factors affect differences between the scales at higher levels, these are more instructive to analyze. The two passages at reading level 7-8—the literature passage from *The Call of the Wild* and the popular fiction passage from *The Son of Tarzan*—are somewhat parallel in content. Their scores according to the New Dale-Chall Readability Formula are also almost identical. The differences between these passages, then, seem to lie beneath their linguistic similarity.

The popular fiction passage (p. 27) details the pain of Korak's loss; his grief is intense but uncomplicated. Ape-man though he is, we can readily identify with his human emotions. On the other hand, the grief of Buck, the wild dog (p. 22), is complicated by a feeling of pride in himself and by his recognition that his master's death is also a liberation from human claims. Understanding Buck's experience requires more imaginative stretch by the reader, as well as a broader consideration of values. The moral universe of literature is generally less circumscribed and conventional than the moral universe of popular fiction. Finally, the linguistic difficulty of the popular fiction passage is related quite directly to vocabulary familiarity, while in the literature passage some uncommon usages of common words may not yield up their full meaning on a first reading: the thought of "death... as a passing out and away from the lives of the living," and the image of moonlight as "ghostly day." Re-readings of the literature passage may thus heighten our awareness of its aesthetic and philosophic dimensions and of its true complexity. Re-reading the popular fiction passage, on the other hand, would seem mainly to repeat our initial impression because there are not multiple layers of meaning to be exposed.

Some differences between literature and popular fiction may indeed be more evident when we consider the effects of re-readings. The popular fiction passages yield little upon re-readings: their messages are more explicit, and their language more conventional, serving mainly as a vehicle rather than as an art form in itself. Literature, as an art, conveys its meanings both implicitly and explicitly; thus re-readings generate further resonances of meaning.

The other side of literature's capacity to yield more to the reader is its heightened demands on the reader. Popular fiction, on the other hand, tends to represent either everyday experiences that appeal to a reader's immediate, direct identification with characters and events (as in the passages at reading levels 2 and 3); or to represent worlds very different from our own, whose novelty generally provides more escape value than perspective on the human condition (as in the passages at reading levels 7-8 and 9-10). Popular fiction demands less reflection on experience; it entertains us or keeps us company, but it does not also make us wiser or stretch us.

In summary, the main differences we noted between popular fiction and literature lie along the following dimensions:

1. **Explicitness vs. implication.** What popular fiction has to convey is quite evident on the surface. In contrast to literature, popular fiction uses less figurative language and makes few allusions. Thus the demands it makes on the reader are basically for understanding explicit messages.

2. **Single vs. multiple layers of meaning.** This dimension is closely related to the previous one. A good reader understands more about a piece of literature from further readings of it. Because of its suggestiveness and ambiguity, literature usually cannot yield its full meaning in one reading.

3. **Redundancy vs. conciseness of expression.** Popular fiction is more redundant than literature; a reader missing a point in one sentence or passage can often pick it up in another, so knowledge of unfamiliar words may not be as crucial for comprehension as in the reading of literature which is more concise.

4. **Conventionality vs. individuality and distinctiveness.** Popular fiction is more conventional in its language than literature is; and since its language generally follows expected patterns, a reader need not pay as close attention to it. The moral universe of popular fiction also tends to be more conventional and simple than that of literature. Though a character may waver in a choice, right and wrong are usually clearly delineated for the reader.

Literature and popular fiction can be distinguished in terms of both what the reader must bring to the text to understand it and what the reader can get out of the text. Literature requires more from and yields more to its readers. Popular fiction, however, need not be regarded as merely second-rate literature. Its aims and its satisfactions are distinct.

# Indicators for Deciding Which Scale to Apply to Fictional Materials

There are no hard and fast, easy-to-apply rules to readily distinguish literature from popular fiction. For assessing levels of difficulty, the distinction is less significant at the lower reading levels (1–3). Users should trust their intuitive, overall judgment of whether a work is literature or popular fiction. This judgment doubtless embraces an appreciation of many of the factors mentioned below and those already discussed in this chapter, especially in the preceding section comparing the two scales.

## For the Literature Scale

1. Language that is more artistic, suggestive, and condensed.
2. Works whose interest lies along several dimensions simultaneously, e.g., complex characterization, original style, carefully crafted structure, thematic depth.
3. Works readers would benefit from reading more than once. Works to be savored and pondered; to reflect upon, analyze, and discuss at some length.
4. Books already established as "classics," whether modern, like *Charlotte's Web*, or older, like *Moby Dick*.
5. Books classified in libraries, bookstores and catalogs as "Literature"—although some books classified as "fiction," especially recently published ones, may have the qualities of literature.
6. Works by authors who have published other books regarded as literature. (But this is not always a guarantee.)

## For the Popular Fiction Scale

1. Language that is more conventional and redundant.
2. Works distinguished chiefly by single characteristics, such as humor, a suspenseful plot, colorful but two-dimensional characters, or a didactic message. Romances, murder mysteries, pure adventure stories, and topical humor, to name a few, tend to be works of popular fiction, but there are inevitable exceptions.
3. Works to be read largely for the purpose of gaining fluency in and enjoyment of reading; or for pleasure, escape, or companionship in personal dilemmas.
4. Books that have a wide and immediate appeal. (Of course, this does not disqualify them as literature, provided they possess other qualities as well.)
5. Books classified in libraries, bookstores and catalogs as "Fiction." However, today's "fiction" may become tomorrow's "literature," so each work must be judged on its own merits.
6. Works by authors who have published other books regarded as popular fiction. (But this is not always a guarantee.)

The scales developed for Literature and for Popular Fiction are found in Chapter 4. For each of the two scales, we present the passage in uniform print. The Literature Scale runs from reading level 1 to reading level 13-15 (college level). The Popular Fiction Scale runs from reading level 1 to reading level 9-10.

To give the reader a sense of how the published text actually appears, facsimiles of the original book pages of the literature scale only, at reading levels 1 to 4, are presented in Appendix A, p. 82.

# CHAPTER 6

# The Science Scales: Life Sciences and Physical Sciences

The science passages were obtained from collections in university, public school, and public libraries. Because reading in the sciences implies the reading of general and specific information, we examined sets of textbooks in graded series, scientific source books, and supplementary science readers and trade books.

Early in the selection process we decided that two scales were needed—one in the life sciences and one in the physical sciences—since each seems to represent not only a different branch of science, but also a different type of thought process.

We focused on a specific content area in each scale in order to highlight the changing text characteristics as levels of difficulty increased. The Life Sciences Scale concentrated on the growth and development of frogs; the Physical Sciences Scale concentrated on astronomy.

## Progression of Difficulty

The Life Sciences and Physical Sciences Scales increase in difficulty along linguistic dimensions in similar ways. Vocabulary becomes less familiar and more precise. Sentences become longer and more complex. However, along *conceptual* dimensions, some differences exist. As well as two distinctly different sciences, the two scales also represent two kinds of scientific writing: *descriptive/technical* and *conceptual/theoretical*. Descriptive/technical scientific writing, at its easiest levels, is primarily factual. As it becomes more difficult, it becomes more microscopic, detailed, and technical. This kind of progression is found in the Life Sciences Scale.

As the life science passages increase in difficulty, the descriptions of frogs become more minute, microscopic and detailed, and use more precise, technical, and esoteric vocabulary. But the passages are all descriptions of phenomena that can be touched, observed, explored, and examined.

By contrast, the physical science passages tend to deal with more abstract ideas. The sun, moon and stars cannot be touched; "space" cannot be seen. As these passages increase in difficulty, the subject matter becomes more removed from the reader's experience. At the most difficult levels, the theoretical discussions are highly abstract, dealing with phenomena that are extremely difficult to visualize, as in the explanation of Einstein's theory of relativity. Whereas some readers may be able to understand four-dimensional space with the help of mathematical formulas and many re-readings, the most difficult passages in the physical sciences involve highly advanced knowledge and thought.

At the easiest reading levels (1, 2, and 3), both the life science and physical science passages are descriptive and explanatory. The focus is on the concrete and factual, often drawing upon the reader's everyday experiences. Experiential activities are suggested to the reader: "Have you ever visited a pond? The air is still, you can hear a buzz" (Life Sciences, reading level 1). The words are generally familiar to the reader. When an unfamiliar, more scientific term is used, it is usually explained in familiar words. Similarly, when a more abstract concept is included, it is explained in words and ideas considered familiar to a child: "A planet is a large world that travels around the sun" (Physical Sciences, reading level 2).

At the next reading levels, 4 and 5-6, the science passages still tend to be descriptive and explanatory. The writing continues to draw upon the reader's everyday experiences, but it begins also to refer to information that was probably learned more formally—in school or from prior reading. At these levels, the reader is beginning to use reading to gain new information that could not be acquired through observations and experience alone: "In addition to breathing with its lungs, the frog also absorbs oxygen through the roof of its mouth" (Life Sciences, reading level 5-6).

Sentences are generally simple, but occasionally more complex sentences are evident. Scientific terms are often described and explained within the passage: "The Milky Way galaxy stretches across the sky in the shape of a large wheel. It has many millions of stars in it..." (Physical Sciences, reading level 4). The use of technical terms with exact, specified meanings also begins. Tadpoles cling to weeds with *suckers* and breathe with *gills*. Stars are described as *nova* and *supernova*. Generally the descriptions and explanations continue to focus on or relate to the concrete. Even in descriptions which are more abstract in nature, attempts are made to relate them to the reader's concrete experiences: "Like vacuum cleaners in space, black holes suck up everything around them" (Physical Sciences, reading level 5-6). However, such attempts to make abstract conceptual information concrete sometimes miss the mark when the information described is related to other conceptual information that is beyond a reader's understanding, such as a description of the collapsing core of an exploding star that keeps compressing until the matter crushes itself out of existence.

At reading levels 7-8 and 9-10, the text assumes that the reader has a highly developed linguistic and conceptual knowledge. It is at these levels where the two scales begin to differ considerably. The text becomes either more technical or more abstract. The Life Sciences Scale tends to focus more on technical details and minute descriptions: "The moist skin of frogs and other amphibians contains mucous glands that assist in maintaining the moisture" (Life Sciences, reading level 11-12).

The Physical Sciences Scale tends to reflect a more cognitive-based structure, providing cause and effect and comparisons and contrasts of differing viewpoints. For example, the reader might be given a reason for a phenomenon: "They thought that many pairs of stars were associated with each other by gravitational forces that made them move in orbits around a common point" (Physical Sciences, reading level 9-10). Also, a hypothesis or proof might be suggested: "When they saw these orbital motions, they proved that Newton's Law of gravitation operates outside our own solar system" (Physical Sciences, reading level 9-10).

Writing at this level includes longer, more complex sentences, generally with many embedded phrases. Scientific terms, whether specified and technical or more abstract and theoretical, are used at an increasing rate. Often such terms are explained and repeated several times after being introduced.

By reading levels 11-12 and 13-15, the text assumes that readers have high levels of linguistic and conceptual knowledge. The writing tends to be analytic, generally presenting information from a variety of viewpoints. Ideas are often implied rather than explicitly stated, making a high demand upon the reader's prior scientific knowledge and ability to think logically about scientific matters. Vocabulary is highly technical and specific in meaning. Sentences are long and complex, highly embedded with relational and qualifying phrases. Although new technical terms may be repeated, they generally are not explained fully in the context of the discussion. Even in the Life Sciences Scale, where the passages from the lowest to highest levels are consistently more descriptive and explanatory, the reader is expected to make comparisons and solve problems.

At reading level 16+ (college graduate reading level), the reader of scientific writing must bring to the text a highly sophisticated linguistic ability, a high degree of scientific knowledge, and strong cognitive and reading abilities. To understand scientific texts at this level, the reader must be able to make inferences, since scientific theories are presented, discussed, and debated. "It is possible to calculate that, if a frog oocyte (a developing egg cell) had the same number of ribosomat RNA genes as a body cell of the frog, it would take many years—far longer than a female frog lives—to make an egg with so many ribosomes" (Life Sciences, reading level 16+).

# Criteria and Benchmarks

In assessing the difficulty of science materials we considered such factors as vocabulary, sentence length and structure, as well as aspects of conceptual difficulty, the prior knowledge assumed, and organization. Passages were selected first by the judgments of the four-member research team, then subjected to a series of analyses, including reading levels from several classic readability formulas as well as estimates of such qualitative aspects of difficulty as conceptual and cognitive demands, difficulty and density of ideas, and text organization. The final evaluations included students' reading comprehension of the selections, their judgments of the difficulty of the selections, as well as the judgments of difficulty of teachers and school administrators. (See Chapter 8, Results of Reliability and Validity Testing.)

General vocabulary was found to range from concrete words within the realm of the young child's everyday experiences to highly abstract words. Technical terms ranged in difficulty from those used to describe familiar phenomena—such as the metamorphosis of tadpoles into frogs—to esoteric words that presuppose a considerable depth of knowledge, as in the Life Sciences Scale, reading level 13-15.

Sentences also varied in length and in degree of simplicity or complexity. Longer, more complex sentences with many embedded phrases characterized the most difficult passages.

Conceptual difficulty was judged by the degree of prior general and technical knowledge required of the reader and by degree of concreteness or abstractness. Theoretical explanations tended to be more difficult than technical descriptions. Generally, as the conceptual difficulty increased, so did the complexity of the sentences. However, some passages of high conceptual difficulty, especially when presented in textbooks, used simple, short sentences, as if the author were making a special effort to make the text more readable.

Conceptual difficulty was also related to the density of ideas within the passages used. Passages with difficult concepts usually contained many implicit as well as explicit ideas. Thus, scientific writing seems to follow the general pattern of text difficulty—difficult ideas tend to be expressed in difficult words, long and complex sentences, difficult concepts, etc. (see Chall & Dale, 1995).

To place science passages at various difficulty levels, we asked what level of linguistic and conceptual understanding the reader needed to bring to the text. Specifically: How wide a vocabulary? What kinds of sentence structure? What levels of conceptual understanding and prior general and technical knowledge?

Using these criteria, we established benchmarks for the scaled levels. (See Table 6-1, p. 64.)

1. How wide a vocabulary is needed?
- *At reading levels 1, 2, and 3:* Mainly short, familiar words. A knowledge of labels for concrete objects encountered in the child's everyday experiences.
- *At reading levels 4 and 5-6:* A more varied vocabulary but still generally familiar. An awareness of scientific terms for scientific phenomena encountered in everyday living, particularly in a technological society.
- *At reading levels 7-8 and 9-10:* An increasing number of uncommon words, including scientific terms and labels for general scientific phenomena.
- *At reading levels 11-12 through 16+:* A wide vocabulary. An ability to accurately use highly technical, often esoteric terms. A familiarity with the vocabulary used for abstract, theoretical discussions.
2. Familiarity with what kinds of sentence structures?
- *At reading levels 1, 2, and 3:* Generally short, simple sentences, with some compound sentences.
- *At reading levels 4 and 5-6:* Longer sentences, some complex. Some embedding of phrases.
- *At reading levels 7-8 and 9-10:* Longer, more complex sentences, generally with embedded phrases. Sentences reflecting coordinating or subordinating structural forms.
- *At reading levels 11-12 through 16+:* Long, complex, and highly embedded sentences—the kind attained through wide reading of challenging fiction and nonfiction.

**Table 6-1**
What the Reader Needs to Bring to the Text to Read **Science** Materials with Understanding

| Reading Levels | 1, 2, 3 | 4 | 5–6 | 7–8 | 9–10 | 11–12 | 13–15 (College) | 16+ (Graduate) |
|---|---|---|---|---|---|---|---|---|
| **Knowledge of vocabulary** | Mainly familiar words. | Some technical terms related to our technological society. | | Wider use of technical terms with more exact and specified meanings. | | Highly technical and specified science terms. Use of words related to theoretical and abstract thinking. | | Uncommon vocabulary, theoretical and abstract. |
| **Familiarity with sentence structure** | Short sentences and structure. | Somewhat longer and complex sentences and phrases. | | Longer, more complex sentences with more embedded phrases. | | | | Long, highly complex sentences with highly embedded phrases. |
| **Subject-related and cultural knowledge** | Can draw upon everyday experiences. | Draws both upon everyday experiences and information learned from books. | | Requires knowledge gained from observations, demonstrations, experiments, and from books. | | | | High extent of prior scientific knowledge. Knowledge of hypothesis testing. Knowledge of science principles. |
| **Technical knowledge** | None, except that gained from everyday experiences in a technological society. | Some technical vocabulary and explanations. | | Knowledge and use of more specified and exact scientific terms. | | Highly specified and more exact technical and scientific knowledge. | | |
| **Density of ideas** | Ability to deal with a few, often repeated ideas. | Ability to deal with increasing number and density of ideas. | | | | Ability to deal with many, often highly embedded ideas. | | Ability to deal with highly embedded ideas, often inferred. |
| **Level of reasoning** | Concrete, easily demonstrated, observed. | | | Begins to require abstract and theoretical thought. | | Ability to apply abstract and theoretical ideas. | | Highly abstract and theoretical. |

3. What level of conceptual understanding and prior knowledge is needed?

- *At reading levels 1, 2, and 3:* Concrete ideas and knowledge that come from everyday experiences, particularly those related to living in a technological society.
- *At reading levels 4 and 5-6:* Some prior knowledge, but generally the descriptions, definitions, and explanations used by most science texts at these levels can be related to the concrete and therefore understood.
- *At reading levels 7-8 and 9-10:* Ideas that are more abstract and theoretical. More specified and minutely described technical knowledge. Considerable prior knowledge is needed.
- *At reading levels 11-12 through 16+:* Very high levels of abstract, theoretical, and technical knowledge are required. Ability to analyze and synthesize information. Knowledge of model building and hypothesis testing as well as the ability to apply scientific principles.

## Development of the Science Scales

For the Life Sciences Scale, we found a wide variety of materials on frogs at the lower reading levels. These tended to be concrete and descriptive. Both textbook and trade book materials written about frogs were plentiful through reading levels 9-10. Beyond this level, passages were less plentiful; the higher level passages were more specific descriptions and explanations of anatomical processes.

For the Physical Sciences Scale, the opposite occurred. We found no passages suitable for the first reading level, and therefore we started the Physical Sciences Scale with reading level 2. Most of the suitable passages were at the highest reading levels. We did find some elementary science textbook series containing suitable physical science materials. However, both life and physical sciences passages at reading levels 4 and 5-6 were difficult to locate. Concepts often seemed to be too difficult for readers at these levels. Although the sentence structure seemed appropriate, vocabulary and concepts were still highly technical, abstract, and insufficiently explained.

## Comparison of the Physical Sciences and Life Sciences Scales

Scientific texts and thought at the lower levels of difficulty are generally not technical. As scientific writing increases in difficulty, two types of structure seem to emerge: the technical/descriptive and the abstract/theoretical. The Life Sciences Scale is an example of the technical/descriptive, whereas the Physical Sciences Scale is an example of the theoretical/abstract.

Technical/descriptive writing, as it increases in difficulty, tends to demand from the reader an increasing technical vocabulary and more extensive and exact knowledge of the subject. As it becomes more difficult, it becomes increasingly explicit and technical in its descriptions and explanations.

Scientific writing of an abstract/theoretical nature requires the reader to possess even more advanced knowledge of specific vocabulary and ideas. The more difficult passages of this type include implied references to underlying theoretical assumptions and related scientific laws.

It should be noted, however, that these differences in scientific writing are not always clearly distinguishable, particularly at the higher reading levels. Theoretical writing often includes technical descriptions, and descriptive articles include hypotheses.

In summary, the degrees of difficulty in the Life Sciences and Physical Sciences Scales generally fall along the following continua:

- **Concrete versus abstract.** The descriptive Life Sciences Scale tends to remain generally concrete throughout, whereas the theoretical Physical Sciences Scale becomes increasingly more abstract.
- **Technical versus abstract vocabulary.** The vocabulary found in the descriptive Life Sciences Scale becomes increasingly more technical, exact, and specified as to its referents. Although the vocabulary used in the theoretical Physical Sciences Scale is also technical and specific, particularly at the higher difficulty levels, it becomes increasingly more abstract. It carries a connotation of being more tentative and at times speculative.
- **Use of subordinating versus coordinating structure.** Although both scales contain passages employing some of each structure, the descriptive technical writings (Life Sciences) tend to follow a subordinating structural form of giving attributes, descriptions, and examples. The theoretical astronomy passages tend to follow a coordinating structural form of cause and effect, differing viewpoints, and comparison and contrast.
- **Explicit versus implicit text.** Although there is no clear-cut differentiation along this continuum between the descriptive and theoretical writing, the Life Sciences Scale tends to become increasingly explicit in description and explanation, whereas the Physical Sciences Scale tends to become increasingly implicit in the use of underlying assumptions and theories.

The scales developed for Life Sciences and Physical Sciences are found in Chapter 4. For each of the two scales, we present the passages in uniform print. The Life Sciences Scale runs from reading level 1 to reading level 16+ (college graduate level). The Physical Sciences Scale runs from reading level 2 to reading level 16+.

# CHAPTER 7

# The Social Studies Scales: Narrative and Expository

The social studies passages on pp. 38-45 were drawn from a variety of textbooks and trade publications. United States history is the broad content area, the settlement and early years of this country's growth the more specific topic addressed. Maintaining a common topic throughout the social studies scales helps explicate the increasing demands placed upon readers.

Two sets of scaled passages are presented: One set represents expository writing, the other narrative writing. The distinction between narrative and expository writing in the social studies—particularly in history—is well known. Indeed, some writers are particularly known and admired for their historical writings as stories. Others tend to prefer using an expository form which focuses more on events and analyses of them. Of course, much writing uses both. For our scales we differentiated those that were mainly narrative and those that were mainly expository.

The Narrative Scale includes passages ranging from reading level 1 to reading level 11-12. The Expository Scale includes passages from reading level 2 to reading level 16+ (college graduate reading level).

## Progression of Difficulty

Within both the narrative and the expository social studies passages, difficulty increases on the linguistic dimensions of vocabulary and sentence length and complexity. Differences are also evident in the density and complexity of ideas. Somewhat less apparent is the increase in cognitive demands, such as the prior knowledge needed by the reader to understand the ideas not specifically explained in the text. Also less apparent are the advanced comprehension strategies—the reasoning, critical thinking, evaluating, and predicting required to understand more difficult writing. This latter dimension of difficulty is also reflected in the intent of the text; whether simply to describe an historical occurrence or whether to involve the reader in arguments, evaluations, or analyses of historical issues.

At reading levels 1 and 2, the lowest levels of difficulty, language tends to be simple, quite informal, and somewhat repetitive. For example, the following repetition occurs in the expository passage at reading level 2. "At first, *there was* the Pilgrim family... *there were* other bigger families... *there were* thirteen colonies at one time." Repeated word strings are also found in the same passage (reading level 2). "There were thirteen colonies at one time. Thirteen families."

Vocabulary at these levels is predominantly familiar, consisting of high frequency words. When content vocabulary is introduced, e.g., *pilgrim, colonies*, it is usually defined in terms of the experiential knowledge of young readers. For example, in the expository passage noted above, *colonies* are called "families."

In passages at the lowest levels of difficulty, historical concepts are related to concepts that are more familiar to children. Concepts are often explained through illustrations rather than through the words. And, in many books, the childhood of historical figures is emphasized.

Sentences in passages at reading levels 1 and 2 are simple and direct. Short sentences predominate in the narrative passages at these levels, although longer sentences are intermixed, perhaps to create a storytelling style with which beginning readers are generally familiar. Short, simple sentences also occur in the expository passage at reading level 2. When sentences are longer, they seem mainly to be compound sentences joined with the conjunction *and*, a conjunction quite familiar to this age group.

Overall, history text that is intended for the primary grades, is descriptive. Its purpose seems to be to familiarize young readers with persons and events of historical significance which may serve as a foundation for later, more complex reading.

In passages representing reading levels 3 and 4, language remains simple but the style shifts from a spoken language to that of more formal written prose. In contrast to the easiest levels where concrete similes are used to relate new ideas to what children know (e.g., comparing colonies to families), the passages at reading levels 3 and 4 use more abstract concepts.

At reading levels 3 and 4, general vocabulary remains fairly simple while more content-related vocabulary including specific dates, names and places is introduced. Definitions of content-related vocabulary are often included in the text, or meaning may be inferred by the surrounding context. In some instances, however, content-related vocabulary is used without definition. Thus, by reading levels 3 and 4, some prior knowledge of history concepts seems to be assumed by the text.

Sentence structure at reading levels 3 and 4 is, in general, fairly simple, although sentences are consistently longer than at lower reading levels.

The purpose of the text at these levels seems to be to describe events and activities, fulfilling an information-giving function. Yet, descriptions are clearly more detailed than at earlier scale levels.

Passages at reading levels 5-6 and 7-8 demonstrate changes from earlier passages in several respects. For example, the style of writing seems more formal. General vocabulary is also more difficult (less familiar and more abstract) and fewer words are defined. Content-related vocabulary is also more extensive and difficult. No longer does the purpose of the text seem to be descriptive. Ideas as well as facts and events are presented, requiring more advanced reading comprehension, application of prior knowledge and critical thought.

Texts on reading levels 9-10 and 11-12 present more than facts. Ideas and concepts are compared, contrasted, and interpreted. Thus, the demands on the readers' knowledge of history, reading comprehension, and general cognitive abilities are considerable. Knowledge of the meanings of words beyond the most common is also expected at these levels.

The passages at these reading levels are clearly more difficult—composed of less familiar general vocabulary, and particularly an increase in the technical vocabulary. At these levels, readers need an extensive knowledge of technical words related to history. They also need to interpret and compare new information in light of knowledge already acquired. At these levels, syntactic complexity also increases; sentences are generally quite long and complex.

At reading levels 13-15 and 16+, the demands intensify further in vocabulary, syntax, and particularly in interpretation. (Indeed, writing of this complexity does not seem to occur often in narration. Therefore, the most difficult passage selected for the Narrative Social Studies Scale is at reading level 11-12. The Expository Scale selections continue through college graduate reading level, 16+.) Both general and content-related vocabularies are extremely difficult at these levels, presenting more unfamiliar and esoteric words with multiple meanings and connotations. Idea density is high. Sentences are long, difficult, and complicated. Readers must consider and react to individual words, constantly interpret information, be aware of relationships, and bring a broad and deep understanding of general and historical knowledge to their reading. Text at these levels does not simply convey general information about history nor does it relate particular facts. Rather, it assumes an active reader who brings strong prior knowledge and keen interest in the study of history and an understanding of how history is constructed.

# Criteria and Benchmarks

Increasing knowledge and skill—in vocabulary and syntax, in general concepts, and in specific knowledge of historical events and contexts—are required of readers of increasingly more difficult social studies texts. An increasing understanding of how history has been reconstructed is also required, as well as increasing ability to think, evaluate, and make judgments.

Using these requirements as criteria, the following benchmarks present the text and reader requirements for the increasingly more difficult scaled levels.

**1. General and Content-related Vocabulary:**
- *Reading levels 1 and 2:* Predominantly easy, familiar, common words of high frequency. Some content-related vocabulary and concepts if they are within the reader's experiential knowledge. If not within experiential knowledge, then explanations in terms of familiar experiences.
- *Reading levels 3 and 4:* Simple, general vocabulary, but of a broader range than at levels 1 and 2. An increasing incidence of content-related terms, some of which are defined or explained in context. Some uses of figurative language.

- *Reading levels 5-6 and 7-8:* General vocabulary relatively more difficult than in the previous levels, and of a greater range. A wider range of content-related terms, and of less common and more abstract historical concepts.
- *Reading levels 9-10 and 11-12:* Difficult and broad general vocabulary. A wide array of subject-related terms representing many abstract ideas.
- *Reading levels 13-15 and 16+:* Extremely difficult general and subject-related vocabulary. Difficult technical and analytical concepts represented by both subject-related and general vocabulary.

2. **Sentence Structure:**

- *Reading levels 1 and 2:* Informal, often repetitive sentences resembling spoken language patterns. Simple and direct sentence construction, of fairly limited length. Descriptive style and clear sequence of events.
- *Reading levels 3 and 4:* Simple language patterns, although more formal than conventional speech. Simple sentence construction, but longer than at previous levels. Descriptive style with more detail than at previous levels.
- *Reading levels 5-6 and 7-8:* Increasingly formal and academic language. Relatively greater occurrence of longer and complex sentences, with phrases and clauses expressing different ideas.
- *Reading levels 9-10 and 11-12:* Formal language structure. Increasing sentence length and complexity. Use of less common connectives, e.g., *however, therefore, nevertheless,* to show more complex relationships between ideas.
- *Reading levels 13-15 and 16+:* Long, difficult, complex sentences. Unexpected structures requiring attention to and evaluation of relationships within and among sentences.

3. **Prior Knowledge of General and Subject-related Concepts:**

- *Reading levels 1 and 2:* Within the realm of children's common experiences. Familiar and concrete general concepts. Content-related concepts explained in terms of young readers' experiences.
- *Reading levels 3 and 4:* Some prior concepts of a general nature; moving away from totally concrete ideas. Expanded content-related ideas, most often concrete.
- *Reading levels 5-6 and 7-8:* Growing abstraction in subject-related concepts. Increasing knowledge of a general nature is presumed.
- *Reading levels 9-10 and 11-12:* The greater density and difficulty of ideas presumes reader's ability to recall, interpret and compare information, some of which is fairly abstract. Considerable knowledge of historical events and contexts.
- *Reading levels 13-15 and 16+:* Broad and deep understanding of historical events and contexts, historical issues and how history is reconstructed by historians. Extensive knowledge of language.

Table 7-1 summarizes the characteristic changes in the narrative and expository social studies passages as they progress in difficulty from reading levels 1 and 2 to college and college graduate levels.

**Table 7-1**
What the Reader Needs to Bring to the Text for Understanding **Social Studies** Materials

| Reading Level | 1 and 2 | 3 and 4 | 5-6 and 7-8 | 9-10 and 11-12 | 13-15 and 16+ |
|---|---|---|---|---|---|
| **Knowledge of vocabulary** | Easy, familiar, highly frequent general vocabulary | Simple, general vocabulary, growing in breadth. | Vocabulary increasing in depth and breadth. | Vocabulary that is more abstract. | Difficult, extremely abstract vocabulary. |
| **Familiarity with sentence structure** | Simple, direct, short sentences. | Generally simple sentences, although somewhat more complex. | Longer sentences of complex construction. | Formal language structure with increasing syntactic complexity. | Long, complex and/or uncommon sentence structure. |
| **Subject-related and general knowledge** | Knowledge of familiar concepts. | Knowledge of some subject-related concepts. | Knowledge of many subject-related concepts representing abstract, historical ideas. | Knowledge of a wide array of subject-related concepts, representing abstract ideas. | Extensive knowledge of difficult subject-related concepts that are highly abstract. |
| **Cognitive density** | Ability to deal with one main idea. | Ability to deal with more than a single idea, but ideas remain closely related. | Ability to deal with several ideas. | Ability to deal with density of ideas interwoven with fewer explicit relationships. | Ability to deal with many different ideas, many of which must be inferred. |
| **Level of Reasoning** | Ability to deal with ideas related to one's own experience. | Can reason primarily about concrete, subject-related concepts and a few general, more abstract ideas. | Has a store of general and specific knowledge. | Ability to define, interpret and compare information, some of which is highly abstract. Uses advanced comprehension skills. | Ability to evaluate and relate ideas within and among sentences. |

# Development of the Scales

Passages considered for inclusion in the two social studies scales were drawn from a variety of textbooks and trade publications representing reading levels typical of texts used from grade 1 to college graduate level. Samples were selected that presented historical information accurately and that represent an acceptable standard of literary quality.

Levels of difficulty were established initially by the independent judgments of the four members of the research team and by the scores from various readability measures—the Spache (1962, 1974) and the original Dale-Chall formulas (1948[1]).

The final selections of the passages for the scales and of the difficulty levels assigned to them were made on a combined basis of the following evaluations: the combined judgments of teachers and administrators, reading comprehension of students, as well as students' judgments of difficulty of the passages. The results of these tests are presented in Chapter 8, Results of Reliability and Validity Testing, and in Appendix B.

Potential passages were assessed initially by the research team. Their judgments were then compared with the scores from several widely used readability formulas. For most passages, agreement between researchers' estimates of difficulty and formula scores was quite high. Generally, differences between the two occurred on passages that included many references to historical names or places, or that used familiar words in a more sophisticated sense (e.g., "the English refused to *give in* to the rebels' demands and threats"). Occasionally, formula scores seemed to overestimate difficulty when unfamiliar words were well defined in the text.

In selecting representative passages, we also considered the prior knowledge and reading comprehension ability required of the reader. In some instances, a history book may be read for a general overview of past events. In others, it might be read for retention of specific facts, dates or names. Or it may be read to solve a problem requiring an understanding of historical concepts and contexts. We also considered the possibility that these tasks might all be required—some perhaps more at one level than another. That is, selections for earlier grades might be read more for facts and general ideas, while selections for the more advanced grades might require more problem-solving and inferential and critical thinking (Chall, 1983, 1996).

We encountered some difficulties in our search for selections at the lowest levels. For example, only a few books seemed suitable for reading level 1. The passages *intended* for students at this initial level—those that featured the appropriate illustrations, type size, and style—seemed too difficult in text content for the level of reading ability,[2] according to the judgments of the research team. We, therefore, began the Expository Scale on reading level 2. The Narrative Social Studies reading level 1 is more appropriate for students in the latter part of first grade.

---

[1] The New Dale-Chall Readability Formula (Chall & Dale, 1995) became available later and was used as a further check on text readability.

[2] It should be noted that at this level, the text could usually be understood by the same children if it were read to them. But since these scales were developed for reading difficulty, they were judged in terms of reading, not listening comprehension difficulty.

The limited pool of passages found for reading level 1 is less surprising if one considers that reading in content areas such as social studies requires some content-related words over and above a general reading vocabulary. For beginning readers who are developing their word recognition and decoding skills, the additional demand of this content-related vocabulary may be an unrealistic expectation.

In contrast, we found an abundance of potential selections that met all criteria—judgment of the research team, readability scores, teacher and administrator judgments of difficulty, and student comprehension scores—to represent reading level 4. The availability of examples at this level may be attributed to the fact that social studies generally becomes a part of the formal curriculum at about 4th grade, when students are developmentally more able to deal with increasing numbers of facts and concepts not within their own immediate experiences in time and place. Also, reading skills typical of students in grade 4 include the ability to recognize and decode a minimum of 3,000 of the most common words in the language, knowledge of the meanings of these words, and considerable fluency in reading. Thus, the reading development of most students in grade 4 makes it possible for them to use reading as a tool for learning new information (Chall, 1983, 1996).

Large numbers of possible social studies selections were also found at reading level 9-10, since United States history is usually studied in the 10th grade.

# Comparison of Narrative and Expository Social Studies Scales

Narrative and expository writing differ in several respects—at the word and sentence levels, at the level of paragraphs, and at the organization level (Stotsky, 1984).

The cognitive demands imposed by narrative and expository social studies text also differ, particularly at higher levels of difficulty. Narrative text in social studies seems to take a more general approach to presenting historical information, even about a particular event. In contrast, expository history texts take a more analytical approach, leading readers to consider cause and effect, to compare and contrast points of view, and to evaluate solutions proposed for the present and future from knowledge of the past. Expository history also uses more difficult, abstract language and a more formal style.

The narrative passage for reading level 2, for example, typifies heroes and events, with considerable use of dialogue. The expository passage for reading level 2 has a more straightforward, direct and factual style.

At reading level 3, the narrative passage presents historical information by relating it to the life of a famous person. Historical events are personalized through the introduction of fictional characters and incidents. The expository passage at the same level, however, presents historical events more directly.

Expository and narrative passages at reading level 4 tend also to vary in the directness of the historical information being conveyed. The narrative passage includes more fictional characters, while the expository passage stays within a contextualized factual account.

The narrative passage at reading level 5-6 continues to personify historical information through fictionalized characters, whereas the expository passage uses an historian's reconstruction of actual events enacted by actual persons.

Throughout reading levels 7-8, 9-10, and 11-12, the same trend appears. Historical facts are personalized in the narrative passages. More information that does not deal directly with history is added.

The narrative scale ends with reading level 11-12. Beyond this level, history text seems no longer to be written as a story.

The scales developed for Narrative Social Studies and Expository Social Studies are found in Chapter 4. For each of the two scales, we present the passages in uniform print. The Narrative Social Studies Scale runs from reading level 1 to reading level 11-12. The Expository Social Studies Scale runs from reading level 2 to reading level 16+ (college graduate level).

# Part IV
Scientific Basis for Qualitative Assessment

CHAPTER 8

# Results of Reliability and Validity Testing

To determine the confidence that could be placed in the qualitative assessment method, we compared the reading levels derived from the scales with various independent measures of difficulty on the same selections. The independent measures included:

1. Rankings of the difficulty levels of the six scales by various groups of teachers and school administrators.
2. Readability levels of passages from children's books and child and adult encyclopedias, using the New Dale-Chall Readability Formula (1995) and the qualitative assessment method.
3. Cloze comprehension tests administered to students, and their judgments of the difficulty of the same selections.

The major findings from the comparisons are presented in this chapter. The detailed findings are presented in Appendix B.

## Comparing Scale Levels with Teacher/Administrator Rankings

Each of the six scales was presented separately to several groups of teachers and administrators. The passages in each scale were presented in a random order of difficulty. As a scale was presented, each teacher and administrator was asked to "rank the passages from easiest to hardest." Criteria for ranking were not given, in order to encourage the use of those normally used when making such judgments. The teachers' and administrators' ranks were compared to those from the four researchers.

Overall, the teachers and administrators agreed with each other and with the rankings of the research team. They also agreed with the student cloze comprehension scores and the student judgments of passage difficulty. In addition, teachers' and administrators' rankings using the qualitative method agreed generally with the levels from widely used readability formulas (Appendix B, Tables B-1 to B-6).

Discussions with these judges after they had ranked the selections for the six scales indicated that the criteria they used varied somewhat. One teacher stressed syntax. She seemed to have been influenced by her dissertation, which was on syntactic features of text. Another was concerned with background knowledge. The passages she ranked as harder, she said, were those that required the reader to have more background knowledge. Still others said they ranked as more difficult those selections that contained harder words or more complex sentences. It is interesting to note that although each judge focused on a different source of difficulty, their rankings were quite similar.

On the whole, judges considered the science passages to be relatively easy to rank because they were more technical, more factual, and had a more technical vocabulary. Most agreed that the easy and hard passages within each scale "pop out at you," while the middle ones are harder to rank. Some teachers were better at ranking than others. Also, as can be seen in Appendix B, there was more agreement on some of the scales than on others.

## Extent of Agreement of Each of the Six Scales

Literature

The teachers and administrators agreed quite well with the research team on the reading levels of the literature passages. Eight of the nine passages in the literature scale had 100% agreement. Only one passage had an agreement of 80 percent. (See Appendix B, Table B-1, p. 92.)

Popular Fiction

The teachers and administrators agreed quite well with the research team in their rankings of the passages. There was close to an 80% agreement for an exact reading level, and close to 100% agreement for ±1 reading level. (See Appendix B, Table B-2, p. 93.)

Life Sciences

Teachers and administrators ranked the life sciences passages on the same reading levels as the research team—from 58% to 83% of the time. When ±1 level was used as the criterion, 83% to 100% of the teachers and administrators agreed with the reading levels assigned by the research team. (See Appendix B, Table B-3, p. 93.)

Physical Sciences

Teachers and administrators ranked the physical sciences passages at the same reading levels as the research team about 67% of the time—ranging from 33% to 92%. When ±1 level was used for the criterion, agreement with the research team's rankings increased to 75–100%. (See Appendix B, Table B-4, p. 94.)

Narrative
Social Studies

The agreement between the teachers' and administrators' rankings and those of the research team on the exact level of each narrative social studies passage was somewhat lower than for the Literature and Popular Fiction Scales. Agreement ranged

---

[1] The lower agreement for the Narrative Social Studies as compared to the Expository Social Studies passages may well be due to the fact that the narrative passages often contained common, familiar words and short sentences (in dialogue) to express rather difficult, sophisticated ideas.

from 50% to 92%.[1] This was also somewhat lower than for the Expository Social Studies Scale. (See Appendix B, Table B-5, p. 94.)

| Expository Social Studies | Overall, there was good agreement on the expository social studies passages between the teachers and administrators and the research team on the exact levels of the passages—from 67% to 100% of the time. The agreement was considerably higher when the criterion was extended to ±1 level—raising agreement to 75% to 100%. (See Appendix B, Table B-6, p. 95.) |

In sum, the various groups of teachers and school administrators were able to rank the passages in an order of difficulty similar to that of the research team. Overall, their ratings were close to those of the research team, particularly when the criterion for *agreement* was defined as the exact level plus or minus one.

# The Validity of Qualitative Assessment for Different Categories of Text

| Children's Trade Books | An experienced reading teacher judged the difficulty of 10 children's trade books using the Literature Scale. Each of the 10 books was also assessed by the Spache or Dale-Chall readability formulas, whichever was appropriate. (See Appendix B, Table B-7, p. 95.)<br><br>A comparison of these estimates of difficulty revealed that for 6 of the 10 books, the qualitative assessments based on the Literature Scale placed the books on the same level as the readability formulas. If we include ±1 level as adequate agreement, then 9 out of the 10 books received the same ratings using the qualitative assessment method and using a readability formula. |

| Children's Encyclopedias | Two teachers independently judged the difficulty of 20 articles from a widely used children's encyclopedia, using the qualitative method. The same 20 articles were assessed with the original Dale-Chall formula. The scale levels assigned independently by the two teachers were quite close—14 of the 20 selections (70%) were assigned the same reading levels. When ±1 level is counted as a reasonable level of accuracy, the two teachers agreed on 20 out of the 20 articles.<br><br>The reading levels assigned to the articles by the two judges were also quite close to the Dale-Chall levels. Judge #1 rated nine of the 20 selections on the same level as the Dale-Chall formula. When a difference of ±1 level was used for the criterion, there was 100% agreement between the scale levels and the formula scores. Judge #2 assigned 16 of the 20 articles the same reading level as the Dale-Chall formula gave. With a difference of ±1 level, there was 100% agreement between the scale levels and the formula scores. (See Appendix B, Table B-8, p. 96.) |

| Adult Encyclopedias | Ten teachers who were enrolled in a reading workshop estimated the difficulty of passages of approximately 100 words from an adult encyclopedia by matching them to |

the appropriate scale levels. The passages were also rated using the original Dale-Chall formula.

Agreement between the qualitative ratings and the readability levels was high. The mean qualitative assessments for all the passages were within one level of the Dale-Chall readability formula scores. (See Appendix B, Table B-9, p. 97.)

## Children's Trade Books

Using the Popular Fiction scale, 800 children's books were assessed by an experienced teacher. The books ranged from reading levels 1 to 9-10. After these judgments were completed, 50 books (approximately 5 books from each level) were rated independently by another experienced teacher.

The inter-rater reliability was high. The two raters agreed on the exact reading level 98% of the time for the 50 books. Essentially similar assessments were made by the two judges independently.

The combined assessments of the two raters were then compared to the readability scores (Spache for levels 1 to 3 and Dale-Chall for levels 4 and above) for the 50 books. Agreement on a single reading level was found for 81% of the 50 books.

# Cloze Tests of Reading Comprehension and Student Judgments of Difficulty Compared with Qualitative Assessments

Qualitative assessments were also compared with student cloze comprehension scores on the same selections. The Expository Social Studies Scale was used for this purpose.

Ten proficient readers in each of 2nd, 5th, and 8th grades—thirty in all—took cloze tests on three selections. The first selection was about one level below their reading ability, the second was on their level, and the third a level above. After completing the cloze tests, they were presented with the same three passages—this time with all the deletions intact—and were asked to tell which of the three they thought was the easiest, which was about in the middle in difficulty, and which was the hardest.

The cloze tests were constructed on the procedures established by Bormuth (1968, 1975), and modified by Almeida (1975) for use with children. We deleted every 7th word. As a reliability check, two sets of cloze passages were prepared for each scaled passage level: one starting the deletions after the 7th word and one starting the deletions after the 10th word. Half the second and eighth graders were tested with one set, and half with the other. The fifth graders completed both sets of cloze passages. Only exact responses for the deletions were scored as correct.

For both the fifth and the eighth graders,[2] results from the cloze tests were in general agreement with the qualitative assessments of the research team and the teachers and administrators. (See Appendix B, Table B-10, p. 97.) The 8th graders, as would be expected, were able to fill in 42% of the deletions on the 7-8 reading level

---

[2] The results for grade 2 were considered invalid because the students did not seem to understand the task. Unfortunately, time did not permit previous training on cloze procedure, and four out of the ten second graders did not complete the test.

passage; 39% of the deletions on the 9-10 reading level passage; and 28% on the 11-12 reading level passage. Based on Bormuth's suggestion that 40% of deletions filled in correctly is generally equivalent to 75% accuracy on a multiple-choice test, it would seem that the cloze tests for the 8th graders are in agreement with the levels found from the qualitative assessments.

The results for the 5th graders are not as clear-cut as those for the 8th graders. However, they too agreed quite well with the qualitative assessments of the research team and the teachers and administrators. The level 4 passage was easy for this group of 5th graders, with 58% of the deletions correctly filled in on the cloze test. The level 5-6 passage seems to be harder than predicted (32% of deletions correct). The level 7-8 passage seems to be on about the same level of difficulty as on the qualitative assessment.

## Student Judgment of Passage Difficulty

As noted earlier, after they took the cloze tests, the students were presented with the same three passages, but with the deleted words restored. They were asked to put them in order of increasing difficulty. Their judgments were, on the whole, similar to their cloze test scores. (See Appendix B, Table B-11, p. 97.) Of the three grade level groups, the 8th graders' judgments of difficulty were closest to the qualitative assessments. The eighth graders ranked the three passages at the same levels as the qualitative assessments, with 70–100% agreement.

The judgments of the fifth graders were also good, particularly on passage 4, with the students' judgments almost 100% in agreement with the qualitative assessments. If we use the criterion of ±1 level, the fifth graders were in agreement with the qualitative scoring 90–100% of the time.

The second graders' judgments, like their cloze tests, were not quite as good as those of the fifth and eighth graders. However, if we extend the criterion to include ±1 level, then most of second graders were also able to rank the passages adequately, with 80–100% agreement. (See Chapter 2, pp. 11-12, for students' comments on why they judged passages as easy or hard.)

## Summary

The tests we conducted, comparing the qualitative assessment method with other methods, indicated that it has good reliability and validity. Reliability was high when the independent qualitative ratings were compared for different teachers, administrators, and researchers. Validity was generally high when qualitative reading levels were compared with student reading comprehension, with readability formula scores, and with independent estimates of difficulty by different judges—teachers, administrators, and students.

# Reproductions of the Literature Passages, Levels 1 through 4

The following pages contain facsimile reproductions of the source pages for the Literature Scale passages from reading levels 1 through 4. This presentation is for the benefit of those who may not be familiar with the overall appearance of texts at the early levels of difficulty.

We do not include facsimiles for reading levels 5-6 or higher, since there is usually little distinction between those levels in terms of type size and style and illustrations.

These reproductions are provided for informational purposes only. They are not intended for use as text exemplars in conducting qualitative assessments. A book's design (type size, page layout, and illustrations) can be misleading in terms of the actual difficulty of the text it contains. Large type and colorful illustrations, for instance, often cause judges to rate text as easier than it actually is. Thus, for greatest accuracy, all qualitative assessments should be made against the appropriate scale presented in Chapter 4.

Literature Scale, Reading Level 1

A train! A train!

A train! A train!

Could you, would you,

on a train?

33

Literature Scale, Reading Level 1 (continued)

Not on a train! Not in a tree!
Not in a car! Sam! Let me be!

I would not, could not, in a box.
I could not, would not, with a fox.
I will not eat them with a mouse.
I will not eat them in a house.
I will not eat them here or there.
I will not eat them anywhere.
I do not eat green eggs and ham.
I do not like them, Sam-I-am.

34

Literature Scale, Reading Level 1 (continued)

Literature Scale, Reading Level 2

Literature Scale, Reading Level 2 (continued)

## CHAPTER 10

### There ARE Bears

Jonathan pushed back the big iron pot and stood up.

There were no bears. But up the path came his father, carrying his gun. And with him were Jonathan's Uncle James and his Uncle Samuel, his Uncle John and his Uncle Peter. Jonathan had never in all his life been so glad to see the uncles.

"Jonathan!" said his father, "what a fright you have given us! Where have you been all this time."

"Coming over Hemlock Mountain," said Jonathan in a small voice. And he ran right into his father's arms.

Literature Scale, Reading Level 3

I saw red.

And before I was able to stop myself, I did something I never meant to do.

I PUT THE MAGIC FINGER ON THEM ALL!

Oh, dear! Oh, dear! I even put it on Mrs. Gregg, who wasn't there. I put it on the whole Gregg family.

For months I had been telling myself that I would never put the Magic Finger upon anyone again—not after what happened to my teacher, old Mrs. Winter.

Poor old Mrs. Winter.

One day we were in class, and she was teaching us spelling. "Stand up," she said to me, "and spell kat."

"That's an easy one," I said. "*K-a-t*."

"You are a stupid little girl!" Mrs. Winter said.

"I am not a stupid little girl!" I cried. "I am a very nice little girl!"

"Go and stand in the corner," Mrs. Winter said.

Then I got cross, and I saw red, and I put the Magic Finger on Mrs. Winter good and strong, and almost at once . . .

Guess what?

*Whiskers* began growing out of her face! They were long black whiskers, just like the ones you see on a kat, only much bigger. And how fast they grew! Before we had time to think, they were out to her ears!

Of course the whole class started screaming with laughter, and then Mrs. Winter said, "Will you be so kind as to tell me what you find so madly funny, all of you?"

And when she turned around to write something on the blackboard, we saw that she had grown a *tail* as well! It was

**4**

## Literature Scale, Reading Level 3 (continued)

HOLD THIS PAGE UP TO BRIGHT LIGHT

Literature Scale, Reading Level 4

78                              SOUP AND ME

along the level. Forward we went. I saw the prow of the barrow drop down, and we were on the hill. The wheelbarrow moved easier and easier. Soup was right. From now on, it was downhill all the way. The wheelbarrow rolled right along, almost as if it knew that its destination was the front door of the Baptist Church.

"Easy as pie," said Soup.

"Pumpkin pie." I giggled and so did Soup.

"With whip cream on it."

"And ginger."

The wheelbarrow picked up speed, so quickly that it sort of kicked up like a whipped horse. I thought the handle was going to rip right out of my fingers.

"Hang on," I said.

"If I can," said Soup.

We were running now, full speed, smack down Sutter's Hill and heading full tilt toward the party. Ahead of us, the giant pumpkin bounced around inside the bin of the barrow. I felt like we'd stolen the moon.

"We're out of control!" yelled Soup.

"Turn it. Do anything, anything!"

"Can't."

The front door of the Baptist Church grew bigger and bigger, rushing toward us like a mad monster. My feet hardly touched the ground. I was too frightened to hang on much longer, yet frightened even more to let loose. Soup was screaming and so was I.

"Stop," wailed Soup.

From the street, there was one step up to the door

Literature Scale, Reading Level 4 (continued)

*Havoc on Halloween*          79

of the Baptist Church. The door was closed. Actually it was a double door, painted red, coming at us like a giant red square. I tried to let go of the handle of the wheelbarrow, but my cramped fingers would not unlace. Just then the one front wheel of the barrow hit the one step, and several things happened in rapid succession. The wheelbarrow, which had a split second earlier been traveling down Sutter's Hill at a hundred miles an hour, stopped with a buck. The pumpkin flew out and straight ahead. Soup and I tripped over the suddenly immobile bin of the barrow. The big pumpkin smashed open both the doors of the Baptist Church, rolling at full steam down the center aisle. The aisle was waxed wood, causing Soup and me to slide on our bellies right behind the pumpkin. Pew after pew flew by.

Events did not stop there.

I didn't see Norma Jean Bissell. But as I hurtled forward toward all the surprised faces, I *did* see Mrs. Stetson. She let out a very loud scream, as though the Devil himself had joined the Baptist Church. Ahead of us, kids were bobbing for apples in a huge tub of water. An adult was among them. Raising his dripping face from the tub of water, with an apple in his mouth, was none other than Mr. Hiram Sutter. The apple fell from his teeth, but his mouth remained wide open in the shock of seeing things racing right at him.

Pins were sticking into me from all angles.

Hitting the little step in front of the altar, the pumpkin leaped high. For a second, it hung in the air like a

# APPENDIX B

# Scientific Basis for the Qualitative Scales

Tables B-1 to B-11 contain the specific findings on the validity and reliability for the six scales—Literature and Popular Fiction, Life Sciences and Physical Sciences, and Narrative and Expository Social Studies.

The major findings on validity and reliability, referencing the data in these tables, were reported in Chapter 8 (pp. 77-81).

**Table B-1**
Agreement of Five Teachers and School Administrators with the Research Team
on Ranking **Literature** Passages by Reading Levels

| Average Reading Level According to Research Team | Percent of Judgments at Same Level as Research Team | Percent of Judgments Within ±1 Level of Research Team |
|---|---|---|
| Level 1 | 100% | 100% |
| Level 2 | 100% | 100% |
| Level 3 | 60% | 100% |
| Level 4 | 60% | 100% |
| Level 5-6 | 100% | 100% |
| Level 7-8 | 80% | 100% |
| Level 9-10 | 80% | 100% |
| Level 11-12 | 60% | 80% |
| Level 13-15 | 100% | 100% |

**Table B-2**
Agreement of Six Teachers and School Administrators with the Research Team
on Ranking **Popular Fiction** Passages by Reading Levels

| Average Reading Level According to Research Team | Percent of Judgments at Same Level as Research Team | Percent of Judgments Within ±1 Level of Research Team |
|---|---|---|
| Level 1 | 83% | 100% |
| Level 2 | 83% | 100% |
| Level 3 | 83% | 100% |
| Level 4 | 83% | 100% |
| Level 5-6 | 83% | 100% |
| Level 7-8 | 50% | 83% |
| Level 9-10 | 50% | 83% |

**Table B-3**
Agreement of Twelve Teachers and School Administrators with the Research Team
on Ranking **Life Sciences** Passages by Reading Levels

| Average Reading Level According to Research Team | Percent of Judgments at Same Level as Research Team | Percent of Judgments Within ±1 Level of Research Team |
|---|---|---|
| Level 1 | 67% | 92% |
| Level 2 | 58% | 100% |
| Level 3 | 67% | 100% |
| Level 4 | 58% | 100% |
| Level 5-6 | 58% | 83% |
| Level 7-8 | 75% | 100% |
| Level 9-10 | 83% | 92% |
| Level 11-12 | 67% | 83% |
| Level 13-15 | 58% | 100% |
| Level 16+ | 67% | 92% |

**Table B-4**
Agreement of Twelve Teachers and School Administrators with the Research Team
on Ranking **Physical Sciences** Passages by Reading Levels

| Average Reading Level According to Research Team | Percent of Judgments at Same Level as Research Team | Percent of Judgments Within ±1 Level of Research Team |
|---|---|---|
| Level 2 | 92% | 100% |
| Level 3 | 67% | 92% |
| Level 4 | 67% | 100% |
| Level 5-6 | 67% | 92% |
| Level 7-8 | 67% | 100% |
| Level 9-10 | 33% | 83% |
| Level 11-12 | 42% | 83% |
| Level 13-15 | *(No data--the original passage was replaced.)* | |
| Level 16+ | 50% | 75% |

**Table B-5**
Agreement of Twelve Teachers and School Administrators with the Research Team
on Ranking **Narrative Social Studies** Passages by Reading Levels

| Average Reading Level According to Research Team | Percent of Judgments at Same Level as Research Team | Percent of Judgments Within ±1 Level of Research Team |
|---|---|---|
| Level 1 | 92% | 100% |
| Level 2 | 58% | 83% |
| Level 3 | 50% | 100% |
| Level 4 | 58% | 92% |
| Level 5-6 | 67% | 92% |
| Level 7-8 | 58% | 92% |
| Level 9-10 | 50% | 92% |
| Level 11-12 | 67% | 100% |

**Table B-6**
Agreement of Twelve Teachers and School Administrators with the Research Team
on Ranking **Expository Social Studies** Passages by Reading Levels

| Average Reading Level According to Research Team | Percent of Judgments at Same Level as Research Team | Percent of Judgments Within ±1 Level of Research Team |
|---|---|---|
| Level 2 | 100% | 100% |
| Level 3 | 83% | 100% |
| Level 4 | 83% | 100% |
| Level 5-6 | 67% | 75% |
| Level 7-8 | 67% | 100% |
| Level 9-10 | 42% | 75% |
| Level 11-12 | 58% | 83% |
| Level 13-15 | 83% | 91% |
| Level 16+ | 83% | 91% |

**Table B-7**
Children's Trade Books Rated by the Literature Scale and Readability Formulas

| | Reading Level As Assessed Using Readability Formula | Reading Level As Assessed Using Literature Scale | Proximity of Qualitative Assessment To Formula Assessment |
|---|---|---|---|
| *Spache* | 1.6 | 1 | = |
| | 1.7 | 1 | = |
| | 1.7 | 1 | = |
| | 2.2 | 1 | ±1 |
| | 3.1 | 3 | = |
| *Dale-Chall* | 4 or below | 2 | *(Not applicable)* |
| | 4 or below | 5 | ±1 |
| | 5-6 | 5-6 | = |
| | 5-6 | 5-6 | = |
| | 5-6 | 4 | ±1 |

**Table B-8**
Qualitative Assessment of Articles from Children's Encyclopedias Compared to Readability Formula Scores

| Article # | Dale-Chall Formula Reading Levels | Reading Level As Assessed by Judge 1 | Proximity of Judge 1's Assessment to Dale-Chall Level | Reading Level As Assessed by Judge 2 | Proximity of Judge 2's Assessment to Dale-Chall Level | Agreement of Judge 1 with Judge 2 |
|---|---|---|---|---|---|---|
| 1 | 7-8 | 7-8 | = | 5-6 | ±1 | ±1 |
| 2 | 7-8 | 7-8 | = | 7-8 | = | = |
| 3 | 7-8 | 5-6 | ±1 | 7-8 | = | ±1 |
| 4 | 7-8 | 7-8 | = | 7-8 | = | = |
| 5 | 7-8 | 7-8 | = | 7-8 | = | = |
| 6 | 7-8 | 7-8 | = | 7-8 | = | = |
| 7 | 9-10 | 7-8 | ±1 | 7-8 | = | = |
| 8 | 9-10 | 9-10 | = | 9-10 | = | = |
| 9 | 9-10 | 7-8 | ±1 | 9-10 | = | ±1 |
| 10 | 9-10 | 9-10 | ±1 | 7-8 | ±1 | = |
| 11 | 9-10 | 9-10 | = | 9-10 | = | = |
| 12 | 9-10 | 7-8 | ±1 | 7-8 | ±1 | = |
| 13 | 9-10 | 7-8 | ±1 | 9-10 | = | ±1 |
| 14 | 9-10 | 7-8 | ±1 | 9-10 | = | ±1 |
| 15 | 9-10 | 9-10 | = | 7-8 | ±1 | ±1 |
| 16 | 9-10 | 7-8 | ±1 | 7-8 | ±1 | = |
| 17 | 9-10 | 9-10 | = | 9-10 | = | = |
| 18 | 9-10 | 7-8 | ±1 | 7-8 | ±1 | = |
| 19 | 9-10 | 7-8 | ±1 | 7-8 | ±1 | = |
| 20 | 11-12 | 9-10 | ±1 | 9-10 | ±1 | = |

**Table B-9**

Qualitative Assessment of Articles from Adult Encyclopedias Compared to Readability Formula Scores

| Passage Number | Dale-Chall Formula Reading Levels | Number of Judges Rating Passage | Judges' Mean Rating | Judges' Mean Rating compared to Formula Levels |
|:---:|:---:|:---:|:---:|:---:|
| 1 | 7-8 | 11 | 7-8 | = |
| 2 | 7-8 | 14 | 7-8 | = |
| 3 | 7-8 | 4 | 7-8 | = |
| 4 | 7-8 | 3 | 7-8 | = |
| 5 | 9-10 | 9 | 7-8 | ±1 |
| 6 | 9-10 | 7 | 7-8 | ±1 |
| 7 | 9-10 | 9 | 9-10 | = |
| 8 | 9-10 | 2 | 9-10 | = |
| 9 | 9-10 | 8 | 9-10 | = |
| 10 | 11-12 | 6 | 9-10 | ±1 |

**Table B-10**

Percentage Correct on Cloze Tests of 5th and 8th Grade Students on Passages of Different Levels* of Difficulty

|  | Reading Level of Passage | | | | |
|:---|:---:|:---:|:---:|:---:|:---:|
|  | 4 | 5–6 | 7–8 | 9–10 | 11–12 |
| Grade 5 | 58% | 32% | 34% | | |
| Grade 8 | | | 42% | 39% | 28% |

\*  As assessed by the research team and teacher/administrator ratings.

**Table B-11**

Comparison of Qualitative Assessments with Student Judgments of Difficulty

| Grade Placement of Students | Reading Level of Passage | | | | | | |
|:---:|:---:|:---:|:---:|:---:|:---:|:---:|:---:|
|  | 2 | 3 | 4 | 5-6 | 7-8 | 9-10 | 11-12 |
| 2 | 40%* (80%) | 50% (100%) | 70% (80%) | | | | |
| 5 | | | 90% (100%) | 50% (100%) | 50% (90%) | | |
| 8 | | | | | 100% (100%) | 70% (100%) | 70% (100%) |

\*  The first set of percentages refers to agreement on exact levels. The percentages in parentheses indicate the percent of agreement within one level (exact level ±1).

# Bibliographic Information on the Scale Passages

## Literature Scale

| Level | Source of passage |
|---|---|
| 1 | Dr. Seuss. *Green Eggs and Ham*. New York: Random House Beginner Books, 1960, pp. 33-34. |
| 2 | Dalgliesh, Alice. *The Bears on Hemlock Mountain*. New York: Charles Scribner's Sons, 1952, pages unnumbered. |
| 3 | Dahl, Roald. *The Magic Finger*. New York: Harper & Row, 1966, p. 4. |
| 4 | Peck, Robert Newton. *Soup and Me*. New York: Alfred A. Knopf, 1975. pp. 78-9. |
| 5-6 | Richter, Conrad. *The Light in the Forest*. New York: Alfred A. Knopf, 1953, p. 174. |
| 7-8 | London, Jack. *The Call of the Wild*. New York: Grosset & Dunlap, 1965 edition, pp. 140-1. Originally published in 1903 by the Macmillan Co., New York. |
| 9-10 | Poe, Edgar Allan. "The Pit and the Pendulum." In *Great Tales and Poems of Edgar Allan Poe*. New York: Washington Square Press, 1970, pp. 304-5. Originally published in 1842 by Carey & Hart, Philadelphia. |
| 11-12 | Conrad, Joseph. *Lord Jim*. Boston: Houghton Mifflin Co., 1958. Originally published by J.M. Dent & Sons, Ltd., London, 1900, pp. 148-9. |
| 13-15 | Melville, Herman. *Billy Budd, Foretopman*. In *Four Short Novels*. New York: Bantam Books, 1959, pp. 264-5. Originally published in 1922-4 by Constable & Co., Ltd., London (in the Standard Edition). Written in 1891. |

# Popular Fiction Scale

| Level | Source of passage |
|---|---|
| 1 | Wiseman, B. *Morris the Moose Goes to School*. New York: Scholastic Book Services, 1970, pp. 5-11. |
| 2 | "Too Much Farley, Too Little Sweater." *Sesame Street Magazine*, March 1979, pp. 14-15. |
| 3 | Blume, Judy. *Freckle Juice*. New York: Dell, 1971, pp. 26-8. |
| 4 | Fitzgerald, John D. *The Great Brain*. New York: Dial Press, 1967, p. 48. |
| 5-6 | Fullbrook, Gladys. *Journey of Enchantment*. New York: Harlequin Books, 1969, pp. 91-2. |
| 7-8 | Burroughs, Edgar Rice. *The Son of Tarzan*. New York: Ballantine Books, 1963. Originally published in 1915 by Frank A. Munsey Co., p. 125. |
| 9-10 | Foster, Alan Dean. *Star Trek Log Eight*. New York: Ballantine Books, 1976, p. 151. |

# Life Science Scale

| Level | Source of passage |
|---|---|
| 1 | Barufaldi, James P.; Ladd, George T.; & Moses, Alice Johnson. *Heath Science, Level 2*. Lexington, MA: D.C. Heath, 1984, pp. 193-5. |
| 2 | Selsam, Millicent E., & Hunt, Joyce. *A First Look at Frogs, Toads and Salamanders*. New York, NY: Walker & Co., 1976, pp. 13-4, 16-7. |
| 3 | Morris, Dean. *Frogs and Toads*, Milwaukee, WI: Raintree Childrens Books, 1977, pp. 20-2. |
| 4 | Rockcastle, Verne N.; McKnight, Betty J.; Salamon, Frank R.; & Schmidt, Victor E. *Addison Wesley Science, Level 4*. Menlo Park, CA: Addison Wesley Publishing Co., 1984, p. 15. |
| 5-6 | Cole, Joanna. *A Frog's Body*. New York, NY: William Morrow Co., 1980, pp. 18-20. |
| 7-8 | Patent, Dorothy Hirshaw. *Frogs, Toads, Salamanders, and How They Reproduce*. New York, NY: Holiday House, 1975, pp. 52-3. |
| 9-10 | *Nature* (Marshall Cavendish Library of Science). New York, NY: Marshall Cavendish Corp., 1989, p. 33. |
| 11-12 | Ford, James M., & Monroe, James E. *Living Systems: Principles and Relationships*, 3rd Ed. San Francisco, CA: Canfield Press, 1977, p. 610. |
| 13-15 | Levy, Charles K. *Elements of Biology*, 3rd Ed. Reading, MA: Addison-Wesley, 1982, p. 338. |
| 16+ | Kirk, David L. *Biology Today*, 3rd Ed. New York, NY: Random House, 1980, pp. 551 & 553. |

# Physical Sciences Scale

| Level | Source of passage |
|---|---|
| 2 | Knight, David. *Let's Find Out About Earth*. New York: Franklin Watts, 1975, pp. 8,11. |
| 3 | Wyler, Rose. *The Starry Sky: An Outdoor Science Book*. Englewook Cliffs, NJ: Julian Messner (Prentice Hall), 1989, pp. 15-16. |
| 4 | Mongillo, John, et al. *Reading About Science*. New York: Webster Division of McGraw-Hill, 1981, p. 66. |
| 5-6 | Dickinson, Terrence. *Exploring the Night Sky*. Ontario, Canada: Camden East, 1987, p. 42. |
| 7-8 | Faufmann, William J., III. *Discovering the Universe*, 2nd Ed. New York: W.H. Freeman, 1990, p. 290. |
| 9-10 | Moche, Dinah L. *Astronomy Today*. New York: Random House, 1982, p. 87. |
| 11-12 | de la Cotardiere, Phillipe. *Larousse Astronomy*. New York: Facts on File Publications, 1986, p. 299. |
| 13-15 | Lederman, Leon M., & Schramm, David N. *From Quarks to the Cosmos: Tools of Discovery*. New York: Scientific American Library, 1989, pp. 172-3. |
| 16+ | Guth, Alan H. "Starting the Universe: The Big Bang and Cosmic Inflation." In James Cornell (Ed.), *Bubbles, Voids and Bumps in Time: The New Cosmology*. Cambridge, UK: Cambridge Press, 1989, pp. 143-4. |

# Narrative Social Studies Scale

| Level | Source of passage |
|---|---|
| 1 | Lowrey, Janette. *Six Silver Spoons*. New York: Harper & Row, 1971, pp. 46-8. |
| 2 | Roop, Peter & Connie. *Buttons for General Washington*. Minneapolis, MN: Carolrhoda Books, 1986, pp. 41-4. |
| 3 | Griffin, Judith B. *Phoebe and the General*. New York: Coward, McCann, Geoghegan, 1977, p. 34. |
| 4 | Avi. *The Fighting Ground*. New York: Harper & Row, 1984, pp. 3-4. |
| 5-6 | Forbes, Esther. *Johnny Tremain*. New York: Dell, 1971, pp. 127-8. |
| 7-8 | Marrin, Albert. *The War for Independence*. New York: Atheneum, 1988, pp. 43-4. |
| 9-10 | Vidal, Gore. *Burr*. New York: Ballantine Books, 1973, pp. 47-8. |
| 11-12 | Griswold, Wesley. *The Night the Revolution Began: The Boston Tea Party, 1773*. Brattleboro, VT: Stephen Green Press, 1972, p.37. |

# Expository Social Studies Scale

| Level | Source of passage |
|---|---|
| 2 | Witty, Paul. *The True Book of Freedom and Our U.S. Family*. Chicago: Children's Press, 1956, pp. 24-7. |
| 3 | Dalgliesh, Alice. *The Fourth of July Story*. New York: Aladdin Books/ Macmillan, 1987. |
| 4 | *Childcraft: The How and Why Library, Holidays and Birthdays*, Volume 9. Chicago: World Book, 1986, pp. 210-211. |
| 5-6 | Fradin, Dennis B. *The New York Colony*. Chicago: Children's Press, 1988, pp. 105-6. |
| 7-8 | Boorstin, Daniel & Ruth. *The Landmark History of the American People, From Plymouth to Appomattox*, Volume 1 (Rev.). New York: Random House, 1987, pp. 55-6. |
| 9-10 | Potratz, Jean. "Loyalists in the American Revolution." *Cobblestone*, Volume 8, Number 8, August 1987, pp. 6-7. |
| 11-12 | Athearn, Robert. *American Heritage Illustrated History of the United States—Volume 3: The Revolution*. New York: Choice Publishing, 1988, pp. 189-90. |
| 13-15 | Henretta, James A., & Nobles, Gregory H. *Evolution and Revolution: American Society, 1600-1820*. Lexington, MA: D.C. Heath, 1987, p.248. |
| 16+ | Kendall, Willmoore & Nellie. *Willmoore Kendall Contra Mundum*. New York: Arlington House, 1971, p. 80. |

# REFERENCES

Almeida, P.M. (1975). *Practical implications of the Cloze test for placement in instructional materials.* Unpublished doctoral dissertation, Harvard Graduate School of Education, Cambridge, MA.

Anderson, R.C., Wilkinson, I.A.G., & Mason, J.M. (1991). A microanalysis of the small-group, guided reading lesson: Effects of an emphasis on global story meaning. *Reading Research Quarterly, 26,* 417-441.

Auerbach, I.T. (1971). *Analysis of standardized reading comprehension tests.* Unpublished doctoral dissertation, Harvard Graduate School of Education, Cambridge, MA.

Bodgan, D., & Straw, S.B. (Eds.) (1990). *Beyond communication: Reading comprehension and criticism.* Portsmouth, NH: Boynton/Cook-Heinemann.

Bormuth, J. (1969). The Cloze readability procedure. *Elementary English, 45,* 429-436.

Carver, R. (1975-76). Measuring prose difficulty using the Rauding scale. *Reading Research Quarterly, 11,* 660-685.

Chall, J.S. (1947). *Graded reading paragraphs in health education: Readability by example.* Unpublished master's thesis, Ohio State University, Columbus, OH.

Chall, J.S. (1956). A survey of users of the Dale-Chall formula. *Educational Research Bulletin, 35,* 197-212.

Chall, J.S. (1958). *Readability: An appraisal of research and application.* (Bureau of Educational Research Monographs, No. 34). Columbus, OH: Ohio State University Press. (Reprinted by Bowker Publishing Co., Ltd., Epping, Essex, England, 1974).

Chall, J.S. (1996). *Stages of reading development* (2nd ed.). Fort Worth, TX: Harcourt Brace. (1983) New York: McGraw-Hill.

Chall, J.S., & Conard, S. (1991). *Should textbooks challenge students: A case for easy or hard textbooks.* New York: Teachers College Press.

Chall, J.S., Conard, S., & Harris, S. (1977). *An analysis of textbooks in relation to declining SAT scores.* Princeton, NJ: College Entrance Examination Board.

Chall, J.S., Conard, S., & Harris-Sharples, S. (1983). *Textbooks and challenge: An inquiry into textbook difficulty, reading achievement, and knowledge acquisition.* A final report to the Spencer Foundation.

Chall, J.S., & Dale, E. (1995). *Readability revisited: The new Dale-Chall readability formula.* Cambridge, MA: Brookline Books.

Chall, J.S., Jacobs, V., & Baldwin, L. (1990). *The reading crisis: Why poor children fall behind.* Cambridge, MA: Harvard University Press.

Chinn, C.A., Waggoner, M.A., Anderson, R.C., Schommer, M., & Wilkinson, I.A.G. (1993). Situated actions during reading lessons: A microanalysis of oral reading error episodes. *American Education Research Journal, 30*(2), pp. 361-392.

Clay, M. (1985). *The early detection of reading difficulties.* Portsmouth, NH: Heinemann.

Clifford, G.J. (1978). Words for schools: The applications in education of the vocabulary researches of Edward L. Thorndike. In P. Suppes (Ed.), *Impact of Research on Education* (pp. 107-198). Washington, D.C.: National Academy of Education.

Conard, S. (1981). *The difficulty of textbooks for the elementary grades: A survey of educators' and publishers' preferences*. Unpublished doctoral dissertation, Harvard Graduate School of Education, Cambridge, MA.

Dale, E., & Chall, J.S. (1948). A formula for predicting readability and instructions. *Educational Research Bulletin, 27*, January 21 and February 18, 1948, pp. 11-20, 28 and 37-54. (Reprinted in pamphlet *Readability*. Columbus, OH: Ohio State University, 1948).

Dale, E., & Hager, H. (1950). *Some suggestions for writing health materials*. New York: National Tuberculosis Association.

Egoff, S., Stubbs, G.T., & Ashley, L.F. (1969). *Only connect: Readings in children's literature*. New York: Oxford University Press.

Gray, W.S., & Leary, B.E. (1935). *What makes a book readable*. Chicago: University of Chicago Press.

Harris-Sharples, S. (1983). *A study of the "match" between student reading ability and textbook difficulty during classroom instruction*. Unpublished doctoral dissertation, Harvard Graduate School of Education, Cambridge, MA.

Herber, H. (1978). *Teaching reading in the content areas* (2nd edition). Englewood Cliffs, NJ: Prentice-Hall.

Herber, H.L., & Nelson-Herber, J. (1993). *Teaching in content areas with reading, writing and reasoning*. Boston, MA: Allyn and Bacon.

Klare, G. (1963). *The measurement of readability*. Ames, IA: Iowa State University Press.

Klare, G. (1984). Readability. In P.D. Pearson (Ed.), *Handbook of Reading Research* (pp. 681-744). New York: Longman.

Popp, H., & Lieberman, M. (1977). *A study of the relationships of student achievement to components of reading programs and environmental characteristics*. Final Report to the National Institute of Education, May, 1977, Report No. 400-75-0064.

Porter, D., & Popp, H. (1975). *Measuring the readability of children's trade books*. Report to the Ford Foundation.

Reading Recovery Program (1990). *Reading Recovery booklist*. Columbus, OH: Ohio State University.

Reading Report Card (1985). *Progress toward excellence in our schools: Trends in reading over four national assessments, 1971-1984*. Princeton, NJ: National Assessment of Educational Progress and Educational Service.

*Running Record* (Spring 1992). A newsletter for Reading Recovery teachers.

Shapiro, B. (1967). *The subjective scaling of relative word frequency*. Unpublished doctoral dissertation, Harvard Graduate School of Education, Cambridge, MA.

Singer, H. (1975). The SEER technique: A non-computational procedure for quickly estimating readability levels. *Journal of Reading Behavior, 3*, 255-267.

Smith, D.R., Stenner, J.A., Horabin, I., & Smith, M. (1989). *The Lexile scale in theory and practice: Final report for NIH grant HD-19448*. New Orleans, LA: International Reading Association.

Spache, G.D. (1974). The Spache readability formula. In Spache, G.D., (Ed.), *Good reading for poor readers*. Champaign, IL: Garrard Publishing Company.

Stenner, J.A., Horabin, I., Smith, D.R., & Smith, M. (1988). *The Lexile framework*. Durham, NC: MetaMetrics, Inc.

Stephens, D. (1991). *Research on whole language*. Katonak, NY: Richard C. Owen Publishers, Inc.

Sticht, T.G. (Ed.). (1975). *Reading for work*. Alexandria, VA: Human Resources Research Organization.

Sticht, T.G. (1982). Literacy at work. In B. Hutson (Ed.), *Advances in Reading/Language Research: A Research Annual, 1*, 219-243. Greenwich, CT: Jai Press.

Stotsky, S. (1984). A proposal for improving high school students' ability to read and write expository prose. *Journal of Reading, 28*, 4-7.

Sutherland, Z. (1980). *The best in children's books.* Chicago: University of Chicago Press.

Thorndike, E.L. (1912). *Handwriting.* New York: Teachers College. (Originally published in *Teachers College Record, 11,* March, 1910).

Thorndike, E.L., & Lorge, I. (1944). *The teacher's word book of 30,000 words.* New York: Teachers College, Columbia University.

Weaver, B. (1992). *Defining literacy levels.* Charlottesville, NY: Story House Corporation.

# INDEX

# ABOUT THE AUTHORS

**Jeanne S. Chall, Ph.D.,** is emeritus professor, Harvard University, Graduate School of Education. She founded and directed the Harvard Reading Laboratory for 25 years.

Dr. Chall has written numerous books and articles, including *Readability: An Appraisal of Research and Application*; *Learning to Read: The Great Debate*; *Stages of Reading Development*; *Should Textbooks Challenge Students? The Case for Easier and Harder Books*, with Sue Conard; and *Readability Revisited: The New Dale-Chall Readability Formula*, with Edgar Dale.

She is a member of the National Academy of Education and the Reading Hall of Fame, and has served on the Board of Directors of the International Reading Association and the National Society for the Study of Education.

She has received many awards, including the American Psychological Association's Edward L. Thorndike Award for distinguished psychological contributions to education; the American Educational Research Association for Distinguished Research in Education; and the International Reading Association Citation of Merit.

**Glenda L. Bissex, Ed.D.,** has been a teacher, a teacher of teachers, and a researcher all her professional life. She is the author of *GNYS AT WRK: A Child Learns to Write and Read* and of the forthcoming *Partial Truths: A Memoir and Essays on Reading, Writing, and Researching*, as well as numerous articles on literacy learning and researching. She is co-editor of *Seeing for Ourselves: Case-Study Research by Teachers of Writing*, growing out of the research course she teaches in Northeastern University's Institute on Writing and Teaching. She also serves as Learning Specialist at Goddard College. She is a member of the National Council on Research in Language and Literacy. Her doctorate is in Human Development and Reading from Harvard; her M.A. and B.A. degrees in English are from the University of Chicago and Radcliffe College, respectively.

**Sue S. Conard, Ed.D.,** was lecturer on Education and Director of the Masters Program for Reading and Language at Harvard University, Graduate School of Education. She was also director of the internship program.

Dr. Conard co-authored *An Analysis of Textbooks in Relation to Declining SAT Scores* and *Should Textbooks Challenge Students? The Case for Easier and Harder Books*.

She conducted research on reading materials and readability, and taught graduate courses and seminars on educational publishing and research and practice in reading. She was a former first grade teacher.

**Susan H. Harris-Sharples, Ed.D.,** is Professor of Education, Wheelock College, Boston, Massachusetts, and coordinator of the undergraduate education programs.

Dr. Harris-Sharples co-authored *An Analysis of Textbooks in Relation to Declining*

*SAT Scores* and was a contributing author to *Should Textbooks Challenge Students? The Case for Easier and Harder Books*. She has done extensive readability work for a leading pharmaceutical company and has been a science teacher and a teacher of first and fourth grades.

She currently is President of the Massachusetts Association of Colleges for Teacher Education and is a member of the Boards of Directors of the Massachusetts Reading Association, and of the Massachusetts Association of College and University Reading Educators. Her honors and awards include the American Association of Textbook Publishers' dissertation research award.

# Other Readability Products from BROOKLINE BOOKS

## READINGS ON LANGUAGE AND LITERACY: Essays in Honor of Jeanne S. Chall

### Lillian R. Putnam, Editor

Colleagues and former students honor the lifetime contributions of Professor Jeanne S. Chall to the field of reading. These fifteen reports represent current thinking at the cutting edges of reading teaching as the country goes through its continuing examination and redefinition of how schools should teach reading. These reports indicate the salience of a swing back to a greater focus on building the phonics and skills base. (1997)

ISBN 1-57129-039-7 • $19.95 SC

## READABILITY REVISITED: The New Dale-Chall Readability Formula

### Jeanne S. Chall & Edgar Dale

The Dale-Chall Readability Formula has been the most widely used and consistently valid method for estimating the difficulty of reading materials since it was published in 1948. In *Readability Revisited*, Drs. Chall and Dale present an introduction and historical overview of the original formula, its purposes and uses over the years, and its relation to other measures of readability. The second chapter presents the new revised formula using a new set of criterion passages, an updated word list, and better rules for measuring the two factors of word familiarity and sentence length. The assessment process combines this revised formula with measures based on the cognitive and structural elements of the written material, the characteristics of the target readers, and the reading purpose. The combination provides a new and powerful tool for assessing and creating written materials for use by teachers, publishers, editors and writers. *Readability Revisited* will remain both a standard reference and a definitive history for years to come. (1995)

ISBN 1-57129-008-7 • $29.95 SC

## MANUAL FOR USE OF THE NEW DALE-CHALL READABILITY FORMULA

### Jeanne S. Chall & Edgar Dale

This manual—excerpted from Chapters 2 and 3 of *Readability Revisited*—presents only the essentials for applying the New Dale-Chall Readability Formula:

- detailed instructions
- worksheets (easily photo-reproducible in this convenient 8½x11 format)
- tables for calculating readability scores
- the complete Dale List of 3,000 Words known to fourth-graders
- examples of text illustrating each reading level from 1 to 16+ (college graduate)

Designed for the convenience of users who wish to apply the formula, but do not need the complete historical and theoretical background provided in the full edition of *Readability Revisited*. (1995)

ISBN 1-57129-012-5 • $14.95 SC

## READABILITYMASTER 2000

### Rod Rodriguez & Ezra Stieglitz, Rhode Island College

Now — calculate readability scores on your computer! Type in the necessary 100-word samples from your text selection, and the computer does the rest. Gives readability scores based on the New Dale-Chall Readability Formula *plus* two other popular measures of reading difficulty, to allow you to cross-check the score. Saves time and energy, making the quantitative calculation of readability very accessible! Package includes 3½" diskette(s) plus manual. (1997)

*PC version:* ISBN 1-57129-031-1 • $29.95
*Mac version:* ISBN 1-57129-038-9 • $29.95